Old Flames *and* A Month in the Country

Old Flames
and
A Month in the Country

SIMON GRAY

faber and faber

LONDON · BOSTON

First published in 1990
by Faber and Faber Limited
3 Queen Square London WC1N 3AU

Photoset by Wilmaset Ltd, Birkenhead, Wirral
Printed in Great Britain by
Richard Clay Ltd, Bungay, Suffolk

Screenplay *Old Flames* © Simon Gray, 1990
Screenplay *A Month in the Country* © Simon Gray, 1990
Adapted from the novel *A Month in the Country*
by J. L. Carr, published by the Harvester Press, 1984

Simon Gray is hereby identified as author of this work
in accordance with Section 77 of the Copyright,
Designs and Patents Act 1988.

CIP data for this book is
available from the British Library

ISBN 0–571–14229–X

CONTENTS

INTRODUCTION

Old Flames is intended as a companion piece, sort of, to my last television film, *After Pilkington*.* In that piece, which could also have been entitled *Old Flames*, a mildly self-regarding Oxford don in his late thirties rediscovers a childhood sweetheart and places himself adoringly at her service, just as he had used to do when he was twelve, she eleven. This later service, however, turns out to involve burying a corpse; posing as a homosexual; drugging the old flame's husband; luring his closest friend into a death trap and, finally, on the discovery that the old flame has grown up into a homicidal maniac, putting her tenderly, and indeed rather reverentially, down. The film concludes with the probability that the old flame's husband, a pushy and two-timing classics don, will eventually take the rap for several murders of which he is, as the credits come up, still completely ignorant – which will certainly teach him a valuable lesson, though I haven't the slightest idea what it might be.

On the other hand the film that is actually entitled *Old Flames* and published here is about chaps, and of the kind of relationship – fashionably described as 'male-bonding' – that used to begin, through beatings and whatnot, in those public schools that people tend to believe no longer exist, but I bet still do. What connects it to *After Pilkington* is that again a mildly self-regarding man (though this time a barrister) in his late thirties finds himself at the centre of violently criminal events (though this time bribery, blackmail, drug-trafficking, embezzlement, manslaughter, so forth) that are again initiated by a long-forgotten figure from his childhood. The moral of the piece – perhaps of *both* pieces, now I come to think of it – is this: 'Whatever you do, don't.'

Of the other script published here, an adaptation of J. L. Carr's novel, *A Month in the Country*, I have only two things to say. One: that I hope it doesn't altogether disgrace its origins. Two: if and where it does, that the fault should be recognized as mine and not Mr Carr's.

Simon Gray, February 1990

* First transmitted on BBC on 11 November 1986 and published by Methuen in 1987.

Old Flames

Old Flames was broadcast by BBC Television on 14 January 1990.
The cast was as follows:

DAVID	Stephen Fry
QUASS	Simon Callow
JACKABOY	Clive Francis
NELLIE	Miriam Margolyes
SOPHIE	Hettie Baynes
CAROLINE	Zoe Rutland
Lighting Cameraman	David Feig
Designer	Don Taylor
Sound	Terry Elms
Costumes	Anna Buruma
Producer	Kenith Trodd
Director	Christopher Morahan

A BBC Television production.

ACT ONE

EXT. CRICKET GROUND. DAY
A game of cricket is in progress. The game is taking place on a large ground between the Amplesides Old Boys and the Metropolitan Police. We see the match in long shot, the Police fielding, two middle-aged men batting, as if from DANIEL's *point of view. Then cut to* DANIEL *at the crease. A montage of his batting with great panache. A series of hooks, cuts, drives, against a fast bowler, a spin bowler, etc. All this observed from the point of view of* QUASS, *in his late thirties, seated on a bench.* QUASS *is plump, unhealthy-looking, and has trouble with his breathing, having to use now and then an asthmatic's inhaler. He is dressed in flannels, a silk shirt, a striped blazer, and a boater on top of what is obviously a wig. Cutting between him and* DANIEL, DANIEL *hitting, running, obviously enjoying himself immensely,* QUASS *watching him impassively, once having to use his inhaler, until* DANIEL *is caught on the boundary.*
Cut to:
JACKABOY: Nice knock, Daniel. Nice *little* knock.
　　(JACKABOY, *the Old Boys' Captain, is padded up. He is an intense man, with spectacles and a commanding manner that is slightly odd and clearly has trouble restraining himself.*)
　　Pity you didn't hold yourself in check a bit. If you had, we might have won.
　　(DANIEL *is at a bench unbuckling his pads. During this, we see from the corner of the camera's eye* QUASS *getting up, beginning to wander, purposively, over to* DANIEL *and* JACKABOY.)
DANIEL: (*Barely suppressing indignation*) Well, I'm very sorry, Jack, but I've always believed one ought to play one's natural game. Especially at this level. I mean, after all, we're merely the Amplesides Old Boys playing one of the Metropolitan Police's worst elevens –
JACKABOY: (*Breaking in*) I know who we're playing and I have personal reasons for wanting to beat the hell out of them! I

don't care which eleven they field – their wives, for all I
care – anything to do with the buggers –
(*Over this shouts of triumph from the field.*)

DANIEL: You're in, Jack, I believe.

JACKABOY: What?
(*He turns, glares at the pitch. We see from their point of view
the various massive Police fielders looking in their direction.*)
(*In a mutter*) All right, you sods. Try and get me!
(JACKABOY *braces himself, stalks towards the pitch.* DANIEL
stares after him in disgust.)

QUASS: (*From the side of the bench*) Excuse me, wasn't that
Jackaboy?

DANIEL: What? (*Seeing* QUASS) Oh, yes. Jackaboy.

QUASS: (*Sitting down*) Odd, isn't it, how one goes on
recognizing people, even people one hasn't seen for what,
over twenty-five years.
(*During this we see* JACKABOY *arrive at the crease, take guard,
and completely miss the first ball, which just misses the wicket.*)
It's not really the looks, is it? It's something in the manner
– (*Has a slight wheezing attack*) – or I suppose the nature.
The something unchangeable that's in all our – um –
(*Wheezes again*). And you're Davenport. Daniel Davenport,
aren't you?

DANIEL: That's right.

QUASS: Quass. Nathaniel Quass. I was at Amplesides. We were
in the same house.

DANIEL: (*Clearly not remembering* QUASS) Oh. I'm afraid I
don't –

QUASS: You were a prefect. And Jackaboy was Head of House.
I don't expect he'd remember me either, though he did
beat me once or twice. So perhaps he'd recognize my rear
end. Especially if it was naked and had stripes on it, eh?
(*He laughs.* DANIEL, *finding this image unattractive, attempts
to smile politely.*)
But you only had cause to speak to me once, I believe.

DANIEL: Really? And what did I say?

QUASS: Well, actually you said, 'Oh dear. Well, one does have
to conform. Or try to. As they say.' And you smiled and
sort of winked. Your life is going well, I imagine, isn't it?

4

(DANIEL *makes to speak, doesn't.*)
I mean, no little stutters or stammers, embarrassing
hiccoughs, wayward mishaps, eh?

DANIEL: You're not by any chance attempting to sell me
something, are you?

QUASS: What? (*Laughs.*) Against stutters and hiccoughs and
mishaps? Oh, I wish I were! I mean, do I look like the kind
of chap who'd have dung delivered to a neighbour's
doorstep?
(*He stares at* DANIEL *intently. Sudden sound of clapping, and
we see from* DANIEL's *point of view* JACKABOY, *his stumps
spreadeagled, walking furiously towards the pavilion ahead of
the other batsman, fielders leaving.*)

DANIEL: (*Rising*) The game's over. And I must get back to the
pavilion.

QUASS: Oh. (*Clearly disappointed*) There was so much I wanted
to – to – but look. I say –
(*Getting up, staring at him almost pleadingly, he reaches into
his pocket, hands* DANIEL *a card.*)
– if ever you want – or need to – well, make contact –

DANIEL: Thank you.

QUASS: I haven't done anything wrong, you know. I've done my
best to – to conform.

DANIEL: Well, that's all any of us can do, really. (*Firmly*)
Goodbye, Mr – um – um – (*Glances down at card.*) Quass.
(*He walks off, slipping the card into his pocket. As he does so,
heading towards the pavilion, he glances back once, and sees,
from his point of view,* QUASS *staring after him, forlornly.*)

INT. CHANGING ROOM. DAY
DANIEL *undressing, along with others, glancing towards* JACKABOY
as he does so. JACKABOY *is sitting by himself, jaw set, staring
furiously down at the floor. The other cricketers are clearly giving
him a wide berth.*

CRICKETER: (*In a mutter to* DANIEL) It was bad enough last
season, when he was just bad-tempered, rude and blustery.
Actually some of us were wondering if you'd have a
word Daniel.

(JACKABOY *suddenly smashes his bat against the ground, gets up, starts to get undressed.* DANIEL *raises his eyebrows, goes over. Other cricketers in and out of shower during this.*)

DANIEL: Everything all right, Jack?

(JACKABOY *looks at him witheringly.*)

JACKABOY: It was a bloody long hop! I was out to a bloody long hop! But it was off a short run. Did you notice that? I think the swine was chucking. But with a fellow cop doing the umpiring – what do you expect, eh?

(*He's now undressed, glaring at* DANIEL.)

DANIEL: Jack, some of the chaps have asked me to have a word with you. They've become rather concerned.

JACKABOY: (*Ignoring him*) Could you hurry with the showers there! (*Going towards the showers*) I've got to get off!

INT. SHOWER ROOM. DAY

A cricketer comes out of the shower; JACKABOY *steps in. We see* JACKABOY *from* DANIEL's *point of view under the shower. A second shower is vacated, and as* DANIEL *makes for it the water in both showers dwindles to a trickle, then gutters out.*

JACKABOY: (*Twisting with increasing savagery at the tap*) What the hell – what the hell! (*To* DANIEL, *intensely*) You know what they've done!

DANIEL: Who?

JACKABOY: The bloody fuzz! They've turned it off at the mains. They've had their showers next door, they're on their way to the pub to swill beer into their bellies – so screw the rest of you, eh?

DANIEL: Well, I don't really think that's likely to be . . .

JACKABOY: I'm meant to be having dinner with Caroline and her parents-in-law. *My* parents-in-law, I mean. Appalling couple.

DANIEL: Can't you have a bath there?

JACKABOY: At the Savoy Grill? (*Throws his towel across the room.*) Oh, those buggers, those buggers!

(*They both begin to get dressed.*)

(*Furiously*) Every time I turn around I find one of them at my elbow – warnings for this, warnings for that, my car

6

clamped, towed away, I even got a wigging for looking up a girl's skirt on the tube – that's what they *claimed* I was doing – I merely happened to glance at her knees – turned out she was a woman cop and the man with her – a brute of a fellow – 'lewd and insulting behaviour' they called it and when I said I'm a gynaecologist, rather a well-established gynaecologist it may interest you to know, she said, 'Well, keep your eyes to yourself when you're not on the job.' Can you believe? And the next day, the very next morning, I got a summons for – where the hell are they? They were here! (*Looking furiously around*) I left them here – *and* my jacket!

EXT. CAR PARK. DAY
DANIEL *and* JACKABOY *are walking rapidly through the car park.*

JACKABOY: What I don't understand is why steal my trousers and jacket, but leave my bag with my wallet and keys. (*Goes to car, looks at watch, stops.*) Do you really think they'll let me in at the Savoy like this? (*Pull back to take him in cricketing flannels and tatty, garish blazer and matching stringy tie.*) I mean – this blazer, what is it anyway? And tie –
DANIEL: I suppose it must be their colours. The police. As we found it in their dressing room.
JACKABOY: (*Gives a bitter laugh.*) Pretentious sods! *And* I stink.
DANIEL: Listen, Jack, I'll give you a call during the week. We'll thrash a few things out about the chaps' feelings – (JACKABOY, *clearly not paying attention, is putting his key in the car door, forcing it.*)
JACKABOY: (*Holding up the key*) It won't bloody turn! (*Looks at the key.*) It's mine all right. These are mine. (*He turns, tries again, then straightens, stands smouldering, then lashes out with his foot at the car door, kicks it in a kind of frenzy.*) (*Shouting in a rage*) Enough, enough, I've had enough, enough – (*A* BURLY MAN *appears carrying cricketing gear, watches this in amazement, then begins to run towards* JACKABOY.)

BURLY MAN: (*Shouting*) Hey – you – hey – stop that, you bloody stop that!

JACKABOY: (*Beside himself*) Bugger off! Mind your own bloody business!

BURLY MAN: I saw you. I saw you kicking the door!

JACKABOY: I'll kick the bloody door any time I want. It's my bloody foot and my bloody door.

BURLY MAN: It may be your bloody foot but that's *my* bloody door!

(*All this is seen from* DANIEL's *point of view. First hesitating, then he begins to sidle away to where his car, a new BMW, is parked.*)

JACKABOY: What?

(*He stares at the car, then looks at the licence plate, then looks further down, spots an identical car.*)

Oh. Right. You're right. Look, I'm sorry. Mine's over there – identical – but I'm in a rush –

BURLY MAN: Oh, are you? In a rush, eh? Look at that door, just look at it – that's malicious damage.

JACKABOY: Malicious damage, what are you talking about? A slight scratch, a dent, all right a dent –

(DANIEL *is now hurrying towards his own car, glancing back occasionally to take in the scene between* JACKABOY *and the* BURLY MAN.)

BURLY MAN: I want a few details. Name, address –

(JACKABOY *takes a wad of money out of his wallet.*)

JACKABOY: Here you are.

(JACKABOY *shoves money at the* BURLY MAN.)

BURLY MAN: What's this?

JACKABOY: What's this? It's money, that's what it is.

BURLY MAN: Are you trying to bribe me?

JACKABOY: Bribe you? I'm giving you some money to pay for the scratch on your door. Don't you understand I'm in a rush, you imbecile?

BURLY MAN: Imbecile. (*Looks at him.*) I should advise you that you're talking to a police officer.

(DANIEL *slides into his car.*)

JACKABOY: A police – oh, of course. Yes. Of course. Hah! Well

– (*Trying desperately to bring himself under control*) – that's only to be expected, isn't it?

BURLY MAN: (*Taking* JACKABOY *in carefully*) What's that you're wearing?

JACKABOY: Eh?

BURLY MAN: That blazer. That tie.

(DANIEL *starts the engine gently as:*)

Where did you get them?

(DANIEL *glides the car out, drives off. As he goes we see* JACKABOY *expostulating furiously as the* BURLY MAN *takes his arm, then struggling, and the* BURLY MAN *fixing him in an armlock, shouting. Two other cops in blazers come running, and we cut to* DANIEL, *his face, his expression shifty but relieved. He opens the glove compartment, and we see from his point of view an assortment of packages of sweets. He takes a sweet out of a package, pops it into his mouth. Last image of* JACKABOY *being frogmarched to car.*)

INT. DANIEL'S HOUSE: LIVING ROOM. NIGHT
We come in on SOPHIE's *face pressed against the sofa, eyes closed, breathing heavily with pleasure, her head moving rhythmically up and down. She is wearing a nightdress which is rumpled up around her shoulders. Mozart from the radio.*

DANIEL: (*Out of shot*) But of course in my position I have to be careful about getting involved with the police. Anyway, I don't really see what I could have done, do you?

SOPHIE: Lovely, lovely, Popsie. 'S all I want. Does for me.

(*Cut to* DANIEL, *his dressing gown open, seeming to be sitting astride* SOPHIE, *his hands on her naked back. He smiles in affectionate reproof.*)

DANIEL: You haven't heard a word I've said, have you, Bootsie?

SOPHIE: Mmmm? Yes, I have. You scored nearly fifty.

(DANIEL *bends over and kisses the top of her head, then gets up.*)

DANIEL: (*Pulling down her nightdress and helping her to sit up*) Come on, let's get you all to bye-byes.

(*Cut to* SOPHIE *blinking, slightly dazed.*)

SOPHIE: Oh, you don't mean you're going to do some work!

DANIEL: *Got* to do some work, Bootsie. So that I'm properly
  prepared for the morning.
  (SOPHIE *nods.* DANIEL *begins to help her to her feet.*)
SOPHIE: (*Then remembering*) Oh, it's on your desk. The letter.
DANIEL: What letter?
SOPHIE: Don't know. One of those special-delivery chaps
  brought it round. Jolly frightening actually in those great
  goggles and gauntlets, standing there thrusting an envelope
  out at you. And you can't hear a word they say.
  (DANIEL *is going towards his study.*)
  Oh, and I heard your telephone ring a couple of times so
  they're probably some messages on the machine.

INT. DANIEL'S HOUSE: STUDY. NIGHT
*Legal books, etc., on shelves, a desk on which there is an answering
machine, telephone and papers, neatly stacked. There is a large
white envelope on the desk. Sound of Mozart continuing over.*
DANIEL *picks up the envelope, begins to open it, and as he does so
opens a drawer of the desk in which there is again an assortment of
sweets. He pops one into his mouth, then notices two messages
signalled on his answering machine, winds them back, plays them,
continues opening envelope as:*

FIRST MESSAGE: (CARPER's *voice over*) Remember, Daniel, it's
  not how we played the game, but whether we won or lost.
  You've lost.
  (DANIEL *looks puzzled.*)
SECOND MESSAGE: (WOMAN PHOTOGRAPHER's *voice over,
  cheerful, lively*) Hello, Daniel Davenport. Congratters on a
  terrific little innings. But the umpire's finger is up and
  you're out! Hit wicket.
  (DANIEL *stands for a moment, then looks up to see* SOPHIE *at
  the door to his study.*)
SOPHIE: (*Yawning*) Who was it?
DANIEL: Just some fools messing about on the answering
  machine. That's the trouble with those things. (*Finishes
  opening the envelope.*) People can't resist being childish –
  (*He pulls a ticket out of the envelope, studies it, perplexed.*)
SOPHIE: Is that an airline ticket?

DANIEL: It does seem to be, yes.

SOPHIE: Where to?

DANIEL: (*Looks.*) Rio de Janeiro.

SOPHIE: (*Suddenly becoming alert*) Rio de Janeiro?

DANIEL: Yes. (*Studying it*) A one way ticket to Rio de Janeiro, economy class. The flight leaves at midnight. Tonight. (*Staring at ticket*) Obviously some dolt of a travel agent has . . .

SOPHIE: (*Smiling but slightly tremulously*) Well, as long as you're not running out on me.

(*Cut to* DANIEL *smiling at her dotingly.*)

DANIEL: How could I, Bootsie, when I need you so much?

(*Cut to* SOPHIE *standing, resplendently pregnant.*)

(*Out of shot*) All of you.

SOPHIE: You know something, you look so beautiful, Popsie.

INT. COURTROOM. DAY

We come straight in on DANIEL *in his barrister's wig.*

DANIEL: My client, Mr Herman, who as you know stands here accused of a very serious charge indeed – (*He gestures. Cut to* HERMAN, *a man in his mid-fifties, prosperous, respectable-looking, in dock.*)

(*Out of shot*) – Mr Herman, about whom you knew absolutely nothing, rings you up out of the blue, arranges to meet you in a pub in Paddington, and without much ado offers you a large sum of money, ten thousand pounds, if you'll burn down a warehouse in Ilford for him. That is your account, isn't it, Mr Parkes?

(*Cut to* PARKES *in the witness box.*)

PARKES: (*As if himself bewildered*) Yes.

DANIEL: Why, do you think?

PARKES: He said because he needed the insurance –

DANIEL: No, I mean why *you*, do you think, Mr Parkes? Why entrust his reputation, his liberty, his whole future, to you? When he'd never even met you before.

PARKES: I don't know. I suppose he made a mistake.

DANIEL: To have entrusted his future to you?

(PARKES *is for a moment at a loss for words.*)

INT. WINE BAR. DAY
We come in on DANIEL, *eating, while glancing at notes on the table.*

CARPER: (*Over*) He's lying, of course.
    (DANIEL *looks up and we see from his point of view* CARPER, *a man in his mid-forties, well dressed, but with an air of indefinable sleaziness about him. He sits down at Daniel's table.*)
    Ask him about Estapona.
    (DANIEL *stares at him.*)
    Ask Parkes how he managed to have a conversation in Paddington with your client when he and his mum were registered in a hotel in Estapona.
DANIEL: (*After a second*) What hotel?
    (*And cut to* QUASS, *watching from across the wine bar. We see from his point of view* DANIEL *and* CARPER, CARPER *talking, then we see, also from his point of view a* MAN *and a* WOMAN *at a nearby table. The* WOMAN *is laughing, taking photographs of the* MAN, *as if practising with the camera. She suddenly swings the camera around, takes several quick photographs of* DANIEL *and* CARPER *talking. Then cut back to* DANIEL's *face.*)
    And you don't want anything for this?
CARPER: Course I do. I want twenty-five thousand pounds. But if you can't manage that, I'll just have to be satisfied with seeing justice done, eh? At least for now.
    (DANIEL *hesitates, studies* CARPER *again, gets up, gathers his notes together, goes towards the door.*)
QUASS: (*Agitated, approaching* DANIEL) Mr Davenport – Mr Davenport – please –
    (DANIEL *turns to him.*)
    (*Urgently*) Nathaniel Quass. We met at the Amplesides Old Boys' cricket match –
DANIEL: Oh, yes. I'm sorry, Mr Quass, I'm due in court.
    (*He hurries out.* QUASS *turns, looks towards* CARPER, *who has gone over to the table with the* MAN *and the* WOMAN PHOTOGRAPHER. *The* WOMAN *swings camera up, takes a picture of* CARPER, *who laughs, sits down beside them.*)

INT. COURTROOM. DAY
We come in on DANIEL.

DANIEL: Now, Mr Parkes. Does the name Estapona mean
anything to you?
(*Cut to* PARKES *looking shifty.*)
PARKES: No, I don't think so.
DANIEL: (*Out of shot, silkily*) It's the name of a seaside resort on
the Costa del Sol, Mr Parkes.

INT. COURT CORRIDOR. DAY
DANIEL, ZELDA (*Daniel's junior*), STRAUSS (*a solicitor*), *coming
out of court into a corridor.*

ZELDA: How did you know?
STRAUSS: Yes, how *did* you know?
DANIEL: Let's just say I found out. Acting on information
received.
STRAUSS: You mean somebody just came up to you and gave
you the name of the village, the name of the hotel, the
exact dates?
DANIEL: Yes.
STRAUSS: Why?
DANIEL: He said he wanted to see justice done.
STRAUSS: A likely story.
(HERMAN *approaches, radiant.*)
HERMAN: Mr Davenport, Mr Davenport –
(*Then, on impulse, he embraces* DANIEL. *And we see from*
DANIEL's *point of view over* HERMAN's *shoulder* PARKES
talking to someone. PARKES *glances at* DANIEL, *gives him an
odd smirking look. The man he is talking to becomes fleetingly
visible. It is* CARPER.)
ZELDA: (*Out of shot*) You're expected in Court Three, Mr
Davenport.
DANIEL: Mmmm?
ZELDA: (*Handing him a brief*) Butley. Receiving stolen goods.
DANIEL: Ah, yes, our Mr Butley.
(*He looks once more quickly at* PARKES *and* CARPER, *then
away.*)

INT. LUIGI'S RESTAURANT. NIGHT

SOPHIE *and* DANIEL *have eaten their meal. On the table are coffee and* petits fours.

SOPHIE: (*Slightly befuddled*) I didn't know you were allowed to do that sort of thing.

DANIEL: My dear Bootsie, it's nothing to do with me if our Mr Herman fixed it with our Mr Parkes and our Johnnie in the wine bar so nothing our Mr Parkes said would be believed, as long as nobody tells me about it. (*Smiles, lifts up* SOPHIE's *hand, kisses it.*) I am merely speculating idly over my birthday dinner – (*Looks lovingly into her eyes*) – with my dear, dear –
(*Piped music begins loudly.* DANIEL *winces, gives an exclamation of disgust.*)
Oh, really, I thought I'd trained him not to.
(DANIEL *turns, looks around as* LUIGI *approaches.*)
Ah, Luigi. (*Smiles reprovingly.*) You put the music on.

LUIGI: Music? Oh, sorry, Signor Davenport, I didn't notice it –

DANIEL: (*Interrupting*) Exactly my point, Luigi. It irritates some of your clients and the others don't even notice.

LUIGI: (*Obsequiously*) I turn it off immediately, Signor Davenport. But I just want to tell you you are wanted on the telephone. A Miss Wright. She say it is urgent.

DANIEL: (*Just suppressing shock*) Miss Wright?

SOPHIE: Who's Miss Wright?

DANIEL: (*Casually, as* LUIGI *turns the music off*) I haven't the slightest idea.
(*He gets up, goes across the restaurant to the telephone, picks it up. We see him keeping an eye on* SOPHIE, *also seeing* SOPHIE *from his point of view sipping coffee, vaguely watching him, beginning to yawn.*)
Hello?
(*Silence on the line, not dead.*)
Davina – (*In a low voice, turning away*) Davina, is that you?
(*There is the sound of someone hanging up.* DANIEL *glances towards* SOPHIE, *and we see from his point of view* LUIGI *going to their table, handing* SOPHIE *something – all of which* DANIEL *doesn't really take in. He dials rapidly. There is a*

*disconnected sound the other end. He hangs up, clearly worried,
goes back to the table.)*
(Hurriedly sitting down) It wasn't for me at all. Well, how
could it be as nobody knew we were here? *(Seeing envelope)*
What's this?

SOPHIE: Luigi brought it over. It arrived by taxi –

*(DANIEL is ripping it open as sounds of 'Happy Birthday to
You' get stronger. DANIEL glances down at the note. Cut to the
note, rapidly seen list of names, some in boxes, some crossed
out, then home in on close-up of sentence:*

> *What is the difference between Miss Wright and Wrong?*
> *Happy birthday, Davenport.*

*'Happy Birthday' now very loud. DANIEL looks up in
bewilderment as LUIGI, leading a gang of waiters, and bearing
a cake with candles on it, is now at the table. They group
around it singing, 'Happy birthday, dear Daniel.' DANIEL,
cramming the letter back into the envelope, clearly completely
unfocused, attempts joviality.)*

DANIEL: Good heavens – well, well. Thank you, Bootsie.

SOPHIE: *(Bewildered)* But it isn't me.

(DANIEL stares at her, then at LUIGI.)

LUIGI: The cake, it came from the taxi driver with the note. He
tell us to surprise you.

SOPHIE: Well, what's in the note?

DANIEL: Nothing. I mean, it just says, 'Happy birthday.' No
name, no signature, nothing. Probably *(Shoving the note into
his pocket)* the girls from chambers – Zelda, Barbara, that
lot. I rather wish they hadn't.

SOPHIE: *(Proudly)* But it shows how fond of you they are,
Popsie.

*(LUIGI gestures towards the candles. DANIEL, attempting a
cheerful manner, sucks in his breath, blows at the candles. They
all seem to go out, to applause from waiters, LUIGI and
SOPHIE.)*

LUIGI, SOPHIE and WAITERS: *(Together)* Bravo, Signor
Davenport, darling, bravissimo, *etc.*

*(And take in, at a distant table, the CAMERA WOMAN and her
COMPANION from the wine bar, looking grinningly towards*

15

DANIEL, SOPHIE, LUIGI, *waiters, grinning and cut to cake. The candles flaming back into life. They are trick candles. And over the shot of candles flickering:*)

ZELDA: (*Voice over, on answering machine*) Hello. A message for Mr Davenport from Zelda Tate. Just to let you know that I've got the Cookson brief. I'll bring it in with me in the morning so you can look at it –

INT. DANIEL'S HOUSE: STUDY. NIGHT

DANIEL *winding forward the answering machine. Take in the sweet drawer, his hand unconsciously taking a sweet and putting it into his mouth. He winds the machine back a little to adjust to:*

MESSAGE: (WOMAN PHOTOGRAPHER'S *voice over*) Hello, Daniel. Dangerous Daniel. I'm calling on behalf of Miss Davina Wright. Or should it be Misdemeanour Wright? (*Slight laugh.*) Happy Birthday.
(*Click.* DANIEL *stops the answering machine, looks up at the ceiling, listening for sounds, then takes out of his pocket the letter he opened in the restaurant. We see it properly:*

> *Coveney*
> *Billington*
> *Cropper*
> *Wardle*
> *Jackaboy*
> *Shulman*
> *Quass*
> *Davenport*
> *What is the difference between Miss Wright and Wrong?*
> *Happy birthday, Davenport.*

DANIEL *studies the list of names. He focuses on* JACKABOY. *He flicks through his address book to Jackaboy, Jack, dials. It is answered almost at once.*)

CAROLINE: (*Voice over, fraught*) Hello.

DANIEL: Oh, Caroline, it's Daniel, Daniel Davenport. I do apologize for – phoning so late, but I have to talk to Jack about something rather important, is he there?

CAROLINE: (*Voice over*) Yes, he's here. But he can't talk now.

(*A strange sound, almost like a laugh.*)
Could you come over, please? He needs your help.
(SOPHIE, *in nightdress, appears at door.*)
DANIEL: (*Registering* SOPHIE) My help?
CAROLINE: (*Voice over*) Please hurry.
(*Click.*)

EXT. JACKABOY'S HOUSE. NIGHT
The front door opens. JACKABOY, *handcuffed, kicking and shouting, is being hustled out by police.* CAROLINE *behind, following. Indecipherable expression on her face as she watches* JACKABOY *being bundled into a police van, driven screechingly off, followed by police car.*
All this seen from DANIEL's *point of view as he sits in his car, clearly having just arrived.* DANIEL *begins to start his car, stops when he sees that* CAROLINE *has seen him.* DANIEL *hesitates, gets out of the car, goes towards her.*

INT. DANIEL'S HOUSE: STUDY. NIGHT
DANIEL *goes to his desk, picks up the list, studies it. Homes in on* QUASS's *name. Not quite able to make it out because of crosses on letters.*

DANIEL: Ass. Ass. Uass. Quass. Quass!
(*He stands, thinking, trying to remember, then remembers, turns, hurries out of the study.*)

INT. DANIEL'S HOUSE: LAUNDRY ROOM. NIGHT
DANIEL *goes to the laundry basket, begins to fumble through it, extracts his cricket trousers, digs into the pocket, and is just pulling out a card when he hears a noise at the door. He turns.* SOPHIE *is staring at him, sleepy but astonished.*

DANIEL: No, no – (*Inspecting his cricket trousers*) – they don't really need washing for Sunday.
(*He surreptitiously pulls the card out of cricket-bags pocket.*)
SOPHIE: Surely Jack didn't call you over just to make sure your cricket flannels –

DANIEL: No, no, of course not. No, I'm afraid Jack is in a spot of trouble. Serious trouble.
(*He slips the card into his trouser pocket.*)

INT. DANIEL'S HOUSE: BEDROOM. NIGHT
SOPHIE *sitting on the bed,* DANIEL *getting undressed.*

DANIEL: (*Continuing undressing*) Caroline says it's – persecution mania – anyway, he's been filing all kinds of complaints and this evening an inspector came around to warn him against wasting police time. An official warning. He had a rather overbearing manner, I expect – but then, of course, Jack's own manner – anyway, he told Jack he was either crazy or a malicious liar. Jack told him he was a liar and a fool. The detective inspector poked him in the chest with his finger. Jack poked him back with a knife. They were in the kitchen. The worst place ever to have a confrontation. Because there are so many to hand. Knives, I mean. And cut him badly in the arm. Pity he didn't try to patch it up.
SOPHIE: Patch it up! After attacking him with a knife!
DANIEL: No, no, patch up the arm, I mean. After all he's a gynaecologist, he can probably put a bandage on, or whatever. Instead he ended up sitting on the detective inspector's face. That's when little Lucas phoned the police – he'd watched the whole thing through the keyhole. Then Caroline came back from her class. Primal-scream class. Then the police arrived. Then I turned up. I suppose the question is whether they'll charge him with attempted murder or GBH. I gave her Quass's name.
SOPHIE: Quass?
DANIEL: Strauss, I mean, the solicitor. Very good chap. Told her I couldn't take the case myself, of course.
(*Cut to* SOPHIE, *sitting, looking worried.*)
SOPHIE: I don't understand, Popsie.
DANIEL: Yes, I know, it's all – all – very unexpected. Jack of all people –
SOPHIE: No, I mean you, Popsie. After all that, how could you then come straight home and check on the state of your cricket flannels?

DANIEL: Yes, I know, Bootsie, but not as odd as it seems. (*Goes into the bathroom.*) I hear that sort of thing every day from the witness box – people who do something – something mundane or routine when in a state of shock.
(*Sound of running water.*)

SOPHIE: Yes, I suppose – when Daddy died Mummy went straight to the henhouse. (*Yawns. Suddenly seeing the telephone*) Oh. Somebody phoned for you. Not on your study number, on our number. Just as I was comfortable at last and beginning to fall asleep –

DANIEL: (*Out of shot, interrupting*) Who was it?

SOPHIE: He had one of those names – Papgood.

DANIEL: (*After a slight pause*) Not, um. Hopjoy by any chance?

SOPHIE: Yes. To say that he might get caught in the traffic in the Mile End Road, but don't worry, he was certain to turn up.
(*Silence from the bathroom.*)
Have I got that right, Popsie? Hopjoy in the traffic.

DANIEL: (*Coming to the bathroom door, not yet seen, trying for nonchalance*) Yes, yes, not that important – not worth phoning late and on the house number –
(SOPHIE *looks at him properly.*)

SOPHIE: What are you doing?
(*Cut to* DANIEL. *He is in his pyjama bottoms, his face covered with shaving cream, holding a razor.*)

DANIEL: Mmmm?

SOPHIE: You're shaving.

DANIEL: Oh, good heavens! My mind was so full of Jack, the poor devil – I mean that I must have thought I was getting up, eh? (*Gesturing and attempting a laugh*) Instead of –

EXT. ELGIN CRESCENT. NIGHT
A girl, DAVINA WRIGHT, *at a window, waving. Cut to* DAVINA *at the window, an expression of horror, not waving but gesturing.*

INT. CAR. NIGHT
Cut to a YOUNGER DANIEL'*s face, also horrified as sound over of soft bump. Stay on his face as we hear again and again the soft*

bump, DANIEL's *face lifting on every bump. Over sound of telephone ringing.*

INT. DANIEL'S HOUSE: BEDROOM. NIGHT
Cut to DANIEL's *face in bed. The telephone ringing continues. Cut to* DANIEL *sitting up in bed, telephone still ringing.* SOPHIE *beside him, snoring.*

DANIEL: (*Picking up the telephone*) Yes?
CARPER: (*Voice over*) Daniel Davenport?
DANIEL: Yes.
CARPER: (*Voice over*) Happy birthday, Daniel. But we mustn't forget absent friends, must we? Like Davina and Geoffrey Hopjoy.
     (*Click.*)
SOPHIE: (*In a slurred voice*) Who is it?
DANIEL: Oh, no one, just some fool. Wrong number.
     (*He lies down, his eyes open, staring.*)

EXT. ELGIN CRESCENT. DAY
Eight in the morning. DANIEL *parking his car. He gets out, hurries up the steps of a house, looks at the row of names under the row of bells. The one he is looking for clearly isn't there. He turns away, perplexed and anxious, and we see coming down the steps of the identical house next door,* DAVINA WRIGHT. *He hurries down the steps so they meet between the two houses.* DAVINA *is in her early forties, pretty, composed-looking, something slightly odd about the composure.* DAVINA *stares at him.*

DANIEL: (*Sickly smile*) Wrong house. (*Gestures backwards.*) I was sure it was fifty-two. But of course it was fifty-four, wasn't it?
DAVINA: (*Smiles brightly.*) Yes, fifty-four. That's where I live. Fifty-four.
DANIEL: I couldn't get you by phone. The number's disconnected –
DAVINA: Oh, yes. I had it disconnected.
DANIEL: Very wise. Given the kind of people who phone one up these days. Was somebody phoning you up?

DAVINA: Oh, no. Nobody at all. That's why I had it taken away. It was so silly waiting for it to ring if nobody was going to ring me.

(*They are walking along the pavement,* DAVINA *rather briskly.*)

DANIEL: I see. But – but it did make it very difficult to return your calls, you see?

DAVINA: Calls? What calls? I haven't made any calls since they took it away. How could I?

DANIEL: You didn't phone me at the restaurant last night or leave a message on my answering machine or have somebody else phone my wife –

DAVINA: Your wife?

(DANIEL *nods.*)

What's her name?

DANIEL: Um – Sophie.

DAVINA: Is she a good wife to you?

DANIEL: Yes.

DAVINA: Yes, she would be. You'd find yourself a good wife, Daniel. And children, have you any children?

DANIEL: No.

DAVINA: I expect you will in due course, won't you? You'll be a good father, Daniel, and your wife Sophie will be a good mother.

DANIEL: Thank you. Um, you haven't phoned her then? Or me?

DAVINA: (*Brightly*) Why should I?

DANIEL: Well, I thought that perhaps you wanted to be in touch.

DAVINA: Our arrangement was that we shouldn't see each other or speak to each other. You shouldn't be here now, Daniel. You shouldn't.

DANIEL: I know. But it is – is an emergency. And nobody has come around asking questions about Geoff?

(DAVINA *looks at him in a sort of shock.*)

(*Gently*) I'm sorry. But I have to know. It's important.

DAVINA: (*Lips trembling*) Nobody's come around asking questions about anything.

DANIEL: And you've never – never told anybody?

DAVINA: You know who I've told, Daniel. Who I have to tell. I tell Him all the time.

DANIEL: (*Thinks, nods.*) But nobody else?

DAVINA: Nobody else. Nobody. Ever. How could I? There isn't anybody else to tell.

DANIEL: (*Nods again.*) Where are you going?

DAVINA: I'm going to Bartholomew's school to watch the children arrive. I do that every morning in term time. Afterwards I go to St Ignatius and sweep the aisles and polish – yes, this morning I shall polish the candlesticks. Then I shall go over to St Mary's, where Father Thomas will find me something to do, I'm sure.

DANIEL: You can't – Davina, you can't live your life in – in a state of – of continual repentance.

DAVINA: I must try.
(*The school is now in sight, with parents and children going in.*)

DANIEL: It wasn't your fault. You had nothing to do with it.
(DAVINA *looks at him brightly.*)

DAVINA: He was my husband. Married in church. A holy service.

DANIEL: Yes. But it wasn't your fault.

DAVINA: (*As if comprehension breaking*) Oh – oh – *that's* why you've come back. To tempt me. Oh, you devil! You *devil!* (*Slaps him viciously.*) Go away, devil! Go away!
(*She slaps him again, turns, walks briskly towards the school.* DANIEL *stares after her, stroking his cheek.* DAVINA *turns, stares at him, screams:*)
Go away, devil! Stop following me, go away!

EXT. DANIEL'S CHAMBERS. DAY
Long shot. DANIEL *hurrying up the steps to his chambers.*

INT. CHAMBERS: LOBBY. DAY
DANIEL *hurrying across the main office, past the receptionist* (BARBARA), *who has an enormous bouquet of flowers which she is unwrapping. We see also peripherally* STRAUSS, COOKSON *and* ZELDA.

BARBARA: (*As* DANIEL *speeds past her desk*) Oh, Mr Davenport,
Mr Davenport –

INT. DANIEL'S OFFICE. DAY
DANIEL *pays no attention, goes straight into his office, strides to his
desk, takes the card out of his pocket, picks up the telephone and is
about to dial when there is a knock on the door.* ZELDA *comes in,
holding the door open.*

DANIEL: (*Sharply*) Yes, Zelda?
ZELDA: Um, Mr Strauss is here with Mr Cookson.
DANIEL: Well then, tell them to wait a moment, will you, I've
    got to make a –
    (STRAUSS *enters with a middle-aged, rather desperate and
    slightly shifty-looking man* – COOKSON.)
STRAUSS: Good morning, Daniel. This is Mr Cookson. Mr
    Cookson, this is Daniel Davenport who is going to be your
    counsel.
    (COOKSON *and* DANIEL *shake hands.*)
DANIEL: Please sit down. Will you – will you excuse me a
    moment? I'll be right back.
    (*He is about to leave. His eye catches the file on his desk. He
    surreptitiously picks it up, goes out of the office.*)

INT. CHAMBERS. DAY
As DANIEL *does so,* BARBARA *is coming towards Daniel's office,
carrying an enormous bowl of flowers, and makes to say something to*
DANIEL. DANIEL *hurries into another office, obviously* ZELDA'S.

INT. ZELDA'S OFFICE. DAY
DANIEL *takes the card out of his pocket, dials.*

QUASS: (*Voice over, cautiously*) Hello, yes.
DANIEL: Can I speak to Nathaniel Quass, please?
QUASS: (*Voice over*) Who is it, please?
DANIEL: Davenport. Daniel Davenport.
QUASS: (*Voice over*) Ah. They've started on you then, have
    they?

DANIEL: Can we meet this evening? The Garrick Club. Seven
o'clock.

QUASS: (*Voice over*) Is it safe?

DANIEL: Of course it is.

(DANIEL *slams down the telephone. He looks at the file in his
hand, runs through it quickly, turning pages, muttering to
himself, braces himself, goes back to main lobby.*)

INT. CHAMBERS: LOBBY. DAY

We see from DANIEL's *point of view* STRAUSS *and* ZELDA *looking
concerned. Then take in* COOKSON *sitting on a chair, sniffing,
dabbing at his eyes with a handkerchief, tears in evidence.* DANIEL
goes over to COOKSON, *who gets up, dabbing at his eyes.*

DANIEL: Come, come, Mr Henshaw, I can assure you the
matter's really not that serious, you know. Even if it comes
to the worst you're only technically a bigamist.

(COOKSON *looks up at him in bewilderment.*)

STRAUSS: Perhaps I could just have a quick word, Daniel?

DANIEL: Mmmm?

(STRAUSS *leads him away. The following is conducted in
urgent whispers.*)

STRAUSS: That's Cookson.

ZELDA: You've got (*Indicating Daniel's file*) the wrong file.
Henshaw's coming in this afternoon. I've got the Cookson
file here –

STRAUSS: (*Interrupting*) Cookson's charged with demanding
money with menaces. Particularly from old ladies living
alone. They haven't got anything, really, apart from some
shaky identification. And a confession. Without the
confession the whole thing would collapse. He claims it was
beaten out of him.

(*Cut to, during this,* COOKSON *snivelling.*)

ZELDA: (*Out of shot*) He was interrogated for fifteen hours
without a break. Pushed around and slapped. One of them,
Cooper, pulled his hair, and the other – Sowerboy –
squeezed his testicles.

STRAUSS: Unfortunately the doctor's report isn't as helpful as
we would like. They were careful not to bruise him.

ZELDA: But there were some scratches around the scrotum.
STRAUSS: Yes, but not incompatible with rough sex,
apparently. He was on his way back from his girlfriend's
when they picked him up.
DANIEL: (*Attempting dignity*) Yes, thank you, thank you. But I
think I'll hear the rest from Mr Dawson direct, if you don't
mind. (*He steps forward.*)
STRAUSS: (*Muttering*) Cookson. The name's Cookson.
DANIEL: (*To* COOKSON) Mr Cookson, I'm sorry about the
earlier confusion. But look, we really can't afford to allow
our – um – emotions to get in the way of our thinking, can
we?
(*He guides* COOKSON *into his office.*)

INT. DANIEL'S OFFICE. DAY
DANIEL: (*Suppressing irritation, as* COOKSON *continues to sniff*)
Do please try and –
STRAUSS: (*From the door*) No, it's the pollen. He has an allergy.
(DANIEL *stares at him blankly, then sees the bowl of flowers
with a card protruding.*)
(*Out of shot*) That's why we came out.
(DANIEL *looks at the card and we see from his point of view:
'Davina and Geoffrey Hopjoy. In memoriam.'*)

EXT. GARRICK CLUB. NIGHT
DANIEL *going up steps. He stops at the porter's lodge.*

DANIEL: I've got a guest arriving in (*he looks at his watch*) half
an hour or so. A Mr Quass.
PORTER: He's already here, sir. He's been here for some time.
He's waiting in the Long Lounge.
(*There is something slightly odd in the porter's manner.*)
DANIEL: Ah. Thank you.

INT. GARRICK CLUB: STAIRS AND LANDING. NIGHT
We follow DANIEL *up through various rooms, men sedately dressed
in sombre-ish suits, one or two in dinner jackets, etc. We see from his
point of view* QUASS *on his hands and knees, groping under an
armchair. An* ELDERLY MEMBER *comes over in front of* QUASS.

QUASS *gets up in disarray. He is wearing a dinner-jacket of exotic design, too big for him, and is in a different wig that fits badly.*

ELDERLY MEMBER: (*Not quite concealing surprise at the spectacle of* QUASS) Is this what you're looking for?
QUASS: Oh yes, how kind. How very kind. Thank you, sir.
ELDERLY MEMBER: Not at all.
(*He withdraws.*)

INT. GARRICK CLUB: LONG LOUNGE. NIGHT
DANIEL *steps forward.* QUASS *sees him.*

QUASS: I arrived a bit early. I hope that's all right.
DANIEL: Oh. And what were you – (*He gestures towards a chair.*)
QUASS: My inhaler. (*Shows it to* DANIEL.) I thought I was going to have an attack, you see. And dropped it.
(*He looks at* DANIEL, *wheezes slightly.*)
DANIEL: But you're all right now, are you?
QUASS: Yes, yes. If I just sit down. May I?
(DANIEL *gestures to the chair, conscious that they are the centre of surreptitious attention.*)
(*Sitting*) Thank you.
(DANIEL *sits.*)
You know what they did today? They sent a whole roast pig to Rabbi Goldman. For his nephew's bar mitzvah. And said it came from me. Is that the kind of thing they've started doing to you?
DANIEL: Along those lines, yes. Did they send you a list?
(QUASS *nods.*)
Did you bring it with you?
(QUASS *takes a list out of his pocket, hands it to* DANIEL. DANIEL *studies it.*)
QUASS: Um – can I see yours, do you think?
(DANIEL *looks at him, then hands over his list.*)
Thank you, Davenport.
DANIEL: They're almost identical – except there are fewer lines and crosses on yours. But the same names in boxes –
QUASS: And on both we're bracketed. As if whatever they're going to do they're going to do to us together.

26

DANIEL: There's no message on yours.

QUASS: No.

(DANIEL *looks at* QUASS, *then takes his list back from* QUASS, *compares the two sheets.*)

DANIEL: Mine is longer. (*Little pause.*) You've cut your message off.

(QUASS *after a second nods.*)

You may have to tell me.

QUASS: Yes, well if I have to I will. As long as you tell me what yours means.

DANIEL: (*Nods.*) Now the first thing to find out is who the others are. What connects us –

QUASS: You mean you haven't realized?

DANIEL: The only name I recognize is Jackaboy's – and now yours.

QUASS: Of course, of course. The rest of us would have been too insignificant, wouldn't we?

(DANIEL *stares at him impatiently.*)

We were all at Amplesides in the same house. I mean I understood that much immediately. In fact it was part of it for me – the nightmare – their names and Jackaboy's particularly. But I suppose we'll have to talk to him, won't we?

DANIEL: Who?

QUASS: Jackaboots. (*Little pause.*) Jackaboy, I mean. Jackaboots is what we used to call him –

DANIEL: We can't talk to him. Not at the moment.

QUASS: Why not?

DANIEL: Because he's gone mad. He's going to be out of circulation for quite a time, I suspect, in gaol or . . .

(QUASS *stares at him apprehensively.*)

QUASS: Oh, dear God!

DANIEL: Have you talked to the others?

QUASS: I've tried to. All of them except Jackab–ab – I didn't have the nerve to phone him. But all the rest. But I only got the wives or mothers or children in one case – Wardle's, I think – and for some reason they were all hostile. I'm not at my best on the telephone – tell me, tell me why do you think it's crosses for Shulman and me, and lines and boxes for the rest of you. I've got a feeling crosses are worse – (*getting slightly shrill*) unless the boxes are tombs –

DANIEL: (*Looking around*) Ssssh.

QUASS: Sorry, Davenport.

(QUASS *wheezes. There is a pause.*)

What's going on then, do you think?

DANIEL: Somebody's trying to mess up my life. That's what's going on.

QUASS: Well, what do we plan to do about it?

DANIEL: Find out who they are and stop them.

SERVANT: (*Approaching*) Mr Davenport.

DANIEL: Yes.

SERVANT: Is your guest Mr Quass?

DANIEL: (*After a pause*) Yes.

SERVANT: He's wanted on the phone, sir. (*To* QUASS) I'll show you where it is, sir.

QUASS: (*Getting up*) I didn't tell anybody I'd be here. Did you?

(DANIEL *shakes his head.*)

Then we were followed.

(*Cut to* SERVANT *and* QUASS *walking off together, watched by* DANIEL. *Cut to* QUASS, *returning, wheezing, agitated. He sits down.*)

(*Nods.*) Them all right. I know the voice. The gruff one.

DANIEL: What did he say?

QUASS: She. It was one of the shes.

DANIEL: Well, what did she say? Come on, Quass.

QUASS: (*Controls wheezing.*) That we're expected at Luigi's. And that you'd know where to go.

DANIEL: Luigi's?

QUASS: Who's Luigi?

EXT. GARRICK: STEPS. NIGHT

QUASS *and* DANIEL *going down the steps.*

QUASS: I told you they find out everything. (*Stops.*) How can you be sure it isn't a trap?

DANIEL: I *know* Luigi. He's almost a friend. And it's a very quiet place.

(*As they talk a pack of Japanese come up the steps, chatting excitedly. They surge around* DANIEL *and* QUASS. DANIEL *takes them in, slightly puzzled.*)

QUASS: But he might not know it's a trap.

DANIEL: (*Looking at the Japanese, smiling to their bows*) Look, Quass, if you're too frightened to come, just say so. I'll go by myself.

(*Cut to* QUASS'*s face, torn by indecision as* DANIEL *strides off.* QUASS *and the last of the Japanese do a kind of dance, attempting to get past each other, then* QUASS *hurries to catch up with* DANIEL.)

INT. LUIGI'S RESTAURANT. NIGHT

The restaurant is completely empty apart from LUIGI *and the* WAITERS *hanging listlessly about, seen from* DANIEL'*s and* QUASS'*s point of view as they enter.* LUIGI *and* WAITERS *straighten hopefully.*

LUIGI: (*Inclining from the hips to* DANIEL) Ah, Signor Davenport, *buona sera* –

DANIEL: (*Tensely, looking around*) Evening, Luigi, I gather you're expecting me.

LUIGI: (*Slightly surprised*) Well, you did book, Signor Davenport.

DANIEL: Right. Good.

LUIGI: (*Glancing towards the door*) And how many will you be altogether?

DANIEL: Don't know really, Luigi, there's a chance somebody else might turn up. If so, you know where I am, bring them over, eh?

LUIGI: Might?

DANIEL: Mmmm?

LUIGI: Somebody might turn up?

DANIEL: Yes. If they do, bring them over.

LUIGI: But you're not sure?

DANIEL: (*Testily*) No, but if they do, bring them over, there seems to be plenty of room.

(*He corrects this with a taut smile, goes over to a table, followed by* QUASS.)

QUASS: (*Looking around*) I see what you mean by quiet.
(*Sudden blast of music.*)

DANIEL: (*Jumps.*) Luigi, Luigi – music!
(LUIGI *adjusts the music until it's even louder, then struts away.*)
What the hell – Luigi – Luigi –

QUASS: (*Terrified*) To cover the noise.

DANIEL: What noise?

QUASS: (*Screeching*) Pistol shots. Screams. It's a trap, I tell you, Davenport.

DANIEL: (*Bellowing*) Luigi!
(LUIGI *comes towards him, smiling.*)

LUIGI: Signor Davenport?

DANIEL: The music, Luigi. You know how I feel –

LUIGI: If I want music in my restaurant, I have music in my restaurant. You don't like it, go eat somewhere else, eh?
(DANIEL *stares at him in disbelief.*)
(*Losing control*) Who do you think you are! You reserve my whole restaurant – my whole restaurant – for the whole evening from seven o'clock, I turn people away, old customers, I cancel reservations and then you come in at nearly nine o'clock and you say, just the two of us, Luigi, somebody might turn up, and you sit down and you tell me, Luigi, off with the music, well, out, get out my restaurant, never again I want to see your face here – eh? Eh? Out, out! Roberto, Angelo, Guiseppe, show these gentlemen the street, show the street –
(*He struts angrily off.*)

INT. DANIEL'S CAR. NIGHT
DANIEL *is driving with just controlled fury with one hand, while from the other he is extracting a sweet from the glove compartment.*

DANIEL: My wife and I have been going there since it opened! We were virtually their first customers! So whatever he was told – however he was tricked – there was no justification – absolutely no justification – for that tone.

QUASS: I know. (*Indignantly*) As if he'd *always* disliked you!
(DANIEL *shoots him a sharp look.*)

(*Hurriedly*) Where shall we go? Shall we go to your place, then?

DANIEL: Of course not. I told my wife I was going out with an important client. How could I possibly explain *you*?

QUASS: (*Shyly*) Well, it'd better be my place, then, hadn't it?

EXT. QUASS'S HOUSE. NIGHT
Daniel's car is parked in the drive. They are standing at the door, QUASS *groping for his keys nervously, conscious of* DANIEL's *eye impatiently on him.*

QUASS: They're here – I know they're here – always in my right-hand pocket – (*Suddenly slaps his forehead*) – of course!
(*He presses the button.*)

NELLIE: (*Voice over, entry phone*) Who?

QUASS: Nathaniel, Nellie.

NELLIE: (*Voice over, entry phone*) Where are your keys?

QUASS: I forgot to take them out of my trouser pocket.

NELLIE: (*Voice over, entry phone*) Well, remember now and take them out. Or aren't you wearing trousers?

QUASS: No, no, I mean when I put on one of father's dinner-jackets, remember. The keys are in my ordinary trousers.

NELLIE: (*Voice over, entry phone*) Just a minute.

QUASS: Nellie, Nellie, where are you going?

NELLIE: (*Voice over, entry phone*) To look in your ordinary trousers.

QUASS: But you don't need my keys. Just press the button I showed you and open the door.

NELLIE: (*Voice over, entry phone*) But how do I know it's you unless I check? You tell me that I have to be careful every time I open the door these days. You'll be furious with me if I let you in and it's not you after all –

QUASS: (*Shouting*) Nellie!

NELLIE: (*Voice over, entry phone*) You wait, Nathaniel, don't be so impatient!
(QUASS *looks at* DANIEL, *whose expression is incredulous, takes him away from entry phone.*)

QUASS: (*Whispering*) I know. She still thinks of me as a child,

she likes to play games – you see, she's a bit, a bit of a
child herself and – and – Of course I haven't told her
anything about all this. She wouldn't understand that
people can be so cruel and I wouldn't want her to
understand –

(NELLIE *opens the door, hands* QUASS *the keys.*)

NELLIE: Now you let yourself in properly like a grown-up
householder –

(*She makes to close the door, sees* DANIEL.)

Oh, my goodness!

QUASS: Yes, Nellie, this is Davenport. Davenport, my sister,
Nellie.

DANIEL: (*Frigidly*) How do you do?

NELLIE: Davenport! This is Davenport! Oh, come in,
Davenport, please.

INT. QUASS'S HOUSE: HALL AND STAIRS. NIGHT

NELLIE: He's talked about you so often, you know, especially
recently, how he's longed to get hold of you again. Come
this way –

(*She leads them through the house, which is opulently
furnished, upstairs, with every so often visible pictures of violin
players.*)

So how was the Mozart, did you bump into each other at
the Mozart?

DANIEL: Yes, that's right. The interval.

INT. QUASS'S HOUSE: LIVING ROOM. NIGHT

*A music stand, expensive hi-fi equipment, television and video,
cassettes, etc.*

NELLIE: (*Opening the door*) Here. Sit. What would you like to
drink, Davenport?

DANIEL: Well – what have you got?

NELLIE: Every cordial under the sun. Made by myself.

QUASS: Nellie, Nellie, offer a proper drink, please. There's malt
whisky, gin, vodka –

NELLIE: Where?

QUASS: In the cupboard in my study.

32

NELLIE: Since when?

QUASS: I got it in last week.

NELLIE: Why?

QUASS: Well, um – (*Embarrassed*) in case we had visitors.

NELLIE: Well, none for you. Cordial for you.

QUASS: (*To* DANIEL) What would you like, Davenport?

DANIEL: Well, actually, a cordial for me too, please.

QUASS: What? Not a Glenfiddich or – Martini, I could make
you a Martini. Or a bloody Mary? (*Pleadingly*) Something
with rum?

NELLIE: You heard him, Nathaniel. There's strawberry,
raspberry, apricot –

DANIEL: Raspberry, please.

NELLIE: (*Triumphantly*) Good choice. For you too, Nathaniel.
(*Goes to the drinks.*) And so you're the famous Davenport
then, such terrible pranks the two of you got up to. My
favourite is the time the two of you climbed through the
house master's window and –
(DANIEL *glances at* QUASS, *who is sitting in acute
embarrassment, half meeting and half avoiding his eye.*)
Ice, Davenport?

DANIEL: Yes, please.

NELLIE: – put glue on his seat so there he stuck – (*Handing*
DANIEL *the drink*) Here, wait, a straw. It's best with a
straw.
(*She hands him a straw.*)

DANIEL: Oh. Thank you.

NELLIE: – and then Nathaniel writing all those poems, the
rhyming ones, to the senior boys, Jackaboots, he was so
happy under your wing. He talks about you in his sleep –
(*Handing* QUASS *his drink*) – you know, Davenport. Only
the other night I heard him shout out –
(*She turns back to* DANIEL.)

QUASS: (*Cutting across*) Nellie, I think Davenport must be a
mite peckish.

NELLIE: (*To* DANIEL) Good. What would you like?

DANIEL: Oh, anything. Anything really.

NELLIE: Then what about sardines in chocolate sauce with
whipped cream on top, eh?

DANIEL: Well –

NELLIE: So why say 'anything', Davenport? Give me an order.

DANIEL: Well, if there were some scrambled eggs, for instance.

NELLIE: With smoked salmon.

DANIEL: Thank you.

NELLIE: For you too, Nathaniel. Only no salt. And, of course, no smoked salmon.

(*She exits. There is a pause.*)

QUASS: Of course you were much on my mind.

(NELLIE *puts her head around the door.*)

NELLIE: Oh, a lot of messages for you, Nathaniel. Mr Rosenblum from the Synagogue Commission very angry, he didn't say why, some people in Lewisham who say thank you for the hundred goat's cheeses, what are they for and can they send them back. And Rabbi Harwood – and the wife of the Yiddish playwright about some turkeys you sent for his first night. Why upset with turkeys – the ones they don't want they can freeze or give away –

QUASS: Please, Nellie, please. Davenport's hungry.

NELLIE: Yes, yes, poor Davenport –

(*She exits.*)

QUASS: Rabbi Harwood! Oh, God, he's a monster! (*Sits trembling.*)
What am I going to do, what am I going to do?

DANIEL: Those phone numbers you said you'd got. Of the others on the list. Where are they?

INT. QUASS'S HOUSE: STUDY. NIGHT

Rather dark, the study gives the impression of mustiness and much use. There is a desk, a telephone (antique) on it, a diary open, with not many entries visible ('Phone Jewish Youth Centre, Lambeth re grant', and 'Phone Shoreditch Jewish Amateur Theatricals: re purchase props', etc.) Otherwise clear. On the wall there is an oil painting of the infant Quass playing a violin. DANIEL *is sitting at the desk, a page of telephone numbers in one hand, the telephone held to his ear by the other. His eye goes to the diary, takes in the entries.*

DANIEL: What do you do?

QUASS: Mmmm?

DANIEL: For a living.

QUASS: Oh, nothing really. Administer a few trusts, charities, Jewish this and that. I've retired, you see.

DANIEL: Retired? At what age?

QUASS: Well, when I left school. Most of this (*Indicating files around the room*) is from my father. He left me certain responsibilities, you see.

(MRS BILLINGTON, *voice over, answers the telephone and gives her number.*)

DANIEL: (*Into telephone*) Oh, hello, can I speak to (*Looks down at sheet*) Mr Billington, please?

MRS BILLINGTON: (*Voice over, telephone*) This is Mrs Billington.

DANIEL: (*Into telephone*) Oh, hello, Mrs Billington. (*Smoothly and confidently*) I'm an old school friend of your husband's, and I was just wondering –

MRS BILLINGTON: (*Voice over, telephone*) He's not here.

DANIEL: (*Into telephone*) Oh, when will he be back, do you know?

MRS BILLINGTON: (*Voice over, telephone*) I've no idea.

DANIEL: (*Into telephone*) I see. Well, thank you very much. (*Hangs up.*) She doesn't know.
(*He dials again.*)

QUASS: Well, at least she was civil with you. When I phoned –
(ROGER COVENEY, *voice over, answers the telephone and gives his number.*)

DANIEL: (*Into telephone*) Is that Mr Coveney?

ROGER COVENEY: (*Voice over, telephone*) No, his son.

DANIEL: (*Into telephone*) Oh, sorry, your voice sounded like your father's. Is he in?
(*Little pause.*)

ROGER COVENEY: (*Voice over, telephone*) Who is it, please?

DANIEL: (*Into telephone*) Just a friend from the old school –

ROGER COVENEY: (*Voice over, telephone*) He's gone away.

DANIEL: (*Into telephone*) Oh, I see. You don't have his number, do you?

ROGER COVENEY: (*Voice over, telephone*) No, goodbye.

DANIEL: (*Into telephone*) Oh. Right, well, thank you – (*Stares at*

35

telephone, clearly having been hung up on.) Apparently his
father has left home. No number.

QUASS: But he told you that much. He refused to speak to me.
(DANIEL *telephones again. Hangs up.*)

DANIEL: Number disconnected.

QUASS: Who?

DANIEL: Wardle.
(*He dials again.*)

QUASS: They were connected last week. Abusive but connected.
Who are you dialling?

DANIEL: (*Dialling*) Shulman.

QUASS: Oh, she was the worst –
(MRS SHULMAN, *voice over, answers the telephone and gives
her number.*)

DANIEL: (*Into telephone*) Oh, hello, can I speak to Mr Shulman,
please?
(*Little pause.*)

MRS SHULMAN: (*Voice over, telephone*) Oh, God.

DANIEL: (*Into telephone*) Is that Mrs Shulman? Well, the thing
is I'm only in London a few days, *en route* from Dubai to
New York, and I suddenly had the urge to look up all my
old school friends, and of course old Shully was top of my
list. We had such times together at Amplesides, we were
known as the Terror Twins, Dangerous Davenport and –
and Suicide Shulman –
(*He laughs.* MRS SHULMAN, *voice over, shrieks.*)
Mrs Shulman, Mrs Shulman, are you there? (*Hangs up.
Looks at* QUASS.) She just let out a sort of shriek and hung
up.
(NELLIE *puts her head in through the door.*)

NELLIE: Scrambled eggs and smoked salmon on the table, boys!

INT. QUASS'S HOUSE: KITCHEN. NIGHT
QUASS *picking at food,* NELLIE *not eating,* DANIEL *gobbling down
his food, a jug of orange squash in front of him to which he helps
himself. He swills, guzzles, swills, guzzles.* DANIEL *is suddenly
aware of their gaze upon him,* NELLIE *nodding proudly.*

DANIEL: I – I hadn't realized quite how hungry I was.

36

NELLIE: But look at Nathaniel, everything on his plate untouched. It's like nursing a sparrow, what a joy it is to have a real forksman in the house at last, so tell me, what is your second name, Davenport?

DANIEL: Um, well, Davenport as a matter of fact.

NELLIE: What! So you're Davenport Davenport? My heavens!

DANIEL: No, I'm Daniel Davenport.

NELLIE: You're Daniel! How come then you always call him Davenport? Just Davenport?

QUASS: Well, at school that's how we called each other, Nellie. I was Quass, he was Davenport –

NELLIE: But now you're grown-ups, call each other Mr Quass, Mr Davenport, or Daniel Nathaniel, why not?
(QUASS *looks at* DANIEL *shyly.*)
I mean, to think I've been going around calling you Davenport –
(*She lets out a scream of laughter.* DANIEL, *almost against his will, lets out a little laugh.* QUASS *laughs with pleasure, but shyly.*)
Now, Daniel, have you finished, what more would you like, plum pie?

DANIEL: Well – well, er – (*Little laugh.*) Thank you.

NELLIE: With a scoop of ice-cream.
(*Cut to* DANIEL *putting in the last spoonful of pudding.*)

DANIEL: That was delicious. Thank you.
(NELLIE *plonks a cup of coffee in front of him, and a bowl with lumps of chocolate in it.* DANIEL *looks at it.*)

NELLIE: Chocolate. Don't be put off by its shape, it's homemade. And now Nathaniel will give you your spiritual pudding. Won't you, Nathaniel?

QUASS: Oh, no. Nellie, really –

NELLIE: Feed the stomach. Then the soul. Would you send him on his way with an empty soul, Nathaniel?

QUASS: (*Seriously*) Nellie, I'm not sure I can.

NELLIE: (*Gently, understandingly*) I think you must try, Nathaniel. I think you must try. (*To* DANIEL, *seriously*) You're a married man, aren't you, Daniel?

DANIEL: Yes.

NELLIE: There, I could tell. And children, have you children?

DANIEL: No – well, yes, my wife is pregnant.

NELLIE: And do you want a boy or a girl?

DANIEL: Well, both actually. She's going to have twins.

NELLIE: Twins! (*Claps her hands.*) So for Daniel's wife and her twins, Nathaniel, you must.

(*Cut to* QUASS's *face as, over, violin music. Then take in* QUASS, *seen full-length from* DANIEL's *point of view, playing the violin, exquisitely. Then take in* NELLIE, *her face aglow with love, watching him, and then take in* DANIEL, *concealing impatience initially, then seduced by the music, popping chocolate into his mouth as he listens.* QUASS, *in a tricky, lyrical passage, eyes closed in concentration. Suddenly his face shows distress. He is clearly having trouble breathing, Doesn't quite get to the end of the passage, stops suddenly in despair, goes to chair and sits down, wheezing, fumbles out his inhaler, recovers his breath before he needs to use it.*)

QUASS: I'm sorry. (*Desolated*) Sorry, Davenport.

(NELLIE *goes to* QUASS, *kneels beside him, pats his hand.*)

NELLIE: No, I'm sorry, my love. Sorry I made you. I was sure it would be all right – (*Turns to* DANIEL.) He would have been a great concert player! A great one! But before an audience it always happens. I hoped that, with such an old friend, it would leave him alone for once. For me every night he plays like an angel.

DANIEL: (*Awkwardly*) Yes, well, um, for me tonight you certainly played – (*Gestures. Glances at his watch.*) Now I really ought to be – um –

(*He looks pointedly at* QUASS.)

INT. QUASS'S HOUSE: STAIRS. NIGHT

QUASS: (*Whispering urgently*) What are we going to do, Daniel?

(*As they get to the front door,* DANIEL *turns.*)

EXT. QUASS'S HOUSE: FRONT DOOR. NIGHT

DANIEL: Something very obvious. Get a private detective, of course. Ask him to check on the names, find out where they are, what's happened to them. It shouldn't take a good one long.

38

(*Above, the sound of the telephone ringing.* QUASS *glances up apprehensively.*)

QUASS: When will you do that?

DANIEL: You'll have to do it. I'm in court tomorrow.

QUASS: But a private detective – how do I know a private detective?

NELLIE: (*Voice over, entry phone*) Nathaniel, Nathaniel, you still down there, Mrs Mossberg is on the phone. To thank you for your present. She sounds very angry.

QUASS: Oh, God, what did I send her!

DANIEL: There's one called Jackson. Frank Jackson. He does a lot of work for solicitors. They say he's very efficient. But of course he'll know my name so don't mention me.

QUASS: How do I get hold of him?

DANIEL: He'll be in the phone book. The moment you find out anything – anything at all – let me know.

NELLIE: (*Voice over, entry phone*) Nathaniel, come now for Mrs Mossberg. Also for your chest. Daniel, send him up straight away.

QUASS: Just coming, Nellie, just coming.

DANIEL: Here's the number of my chamber. (*Scribbling it down on a piece of paper, handing it to* QUASS) They'll know which court I'm in.

NELLIE: (*Voice over, entry phone*) I count to ten, then I come and get you.

DANIEL: Have you got that? the moment you find out anything, get in touch.

(QUASS *nods.*)

Right.

(*He turns, hurries off.*)

QUASS: Good night, Daniel.

INT. DANIEL'S HOUSE: STUDY. NIGHT

DANIEL *enters quietly, turns on desk light, checks for messages on the answering machine. There is one. He opens the sweet drawer, takes out a sweet, and is about to play back the message when he hears a noise from the shadows.* DANIEL *freezes, then very carefully swivels the desk light towards the corner. There is a little cry and simultaneously we take in that the light has hit* SOPHIE, *who has*

*clearly been asleep, full in the face. She is wearing her nightdress,
dressing gown, slippers.*

DANIEL: What are you doing in here, Bootsie?

SOPHIE: (*Drowsy, in a baby voice.*) I always come and sit here
when you're away and I miss you, Popsie. Because it's so
full of you. Do you mind me doing that?

DANIEL: (*Taking her hand*) No, no, of course not, my love.

SOPHIE: And I've been so worried. Where have you been,
Popsie?

DANIEL: Why – with that Turk I told you about, the one who
wants me to defend him on a currency charge. I phoned
you about him, don't you remember me saying I'd be late?

SOPHIE: Of course, I remember. I thought you said he was a
Greek.

DANIEL: Well, yes – but resident in Turkey.

SOPHIE: And you said you were going to have dinner in the
Garrick.

DANIEL: Well, we met at the Garrick. Then decided to go off
somewhere else for dinner. But why, Bootsie, I mean how
did you know that we didn't stay at the Garrick?

SOPHIE: Because they phoned to say you'd left.

DANIEL: The Garrick phoned to say I'd left? Why on earth
would they do that?

SOPHIE: Because they wanted to know where you were.
Apparently there was a little herd of Japanese lawyers
milling about in the entrance hall saying that you'd invited
them to dinner. They even had invitation cards with your
name on it. Apparently it was all a terrible fuss. The man
who spoke to me was really quite angry. Quite rude even,
Popsie.

DANIEL: How – how preposterous! (*Attempts a laugh.*)
Obviously some mistake. Probably confused me with
another Davenport. There're several Davenports at the
Garrick. I'll phone tomorrow and put it right. And I'll
certainly have a word with them about the way they spoke
to you. I won't put up with that sort of thing. But come,
Bootsie, let's get you upstairs to bed.
(*He assists her up.*)

SOPHIE: No, no, play your message.

DANIEL: It can wait.

SOPHIE: No, do it now so you won't have to come down again. Then you can give me a backy rub.
(DANIEL *hesitates, then winds back the tape, plays the message.*)

WOMAN PHOTOGRAPHER: (*Voice over*) Oh, Daniel dear, what is that mess that looks like strawberry jam? Hush, hush, my love, it's poor Hopjoy run over by a – (DANIEL *switches the machine off. Cut to* SOPHIE, *looking bewildered.*)

DANIEL: I told you it was nothing important.

SOPHIE: But who was it?

DANIEL: Just Hopjoy. His way of apologizing for missing our meeting. Got stuck in the traffic, you see.

INT/EXT. CAR. NIGHT
Cut to MAN *lying dead, neck broken, on rear seat. Cut to* DAVINA *in front passenger seat, eyes transfixed. Cut to* DANIEL *behind the wheel, driving in a state of panic,* DAVINA *beside him in a state of shock. He glances into the mirror and we see from his point of view another car in the mirror.*

EXT. MILE END ROAD. NIGHT
Cut to corpse spread out on Mile End Road. Completely silent. Cut to DANIEL *and* DAVINA *in the car, staring towards the corpse. Over the sound of a juggernaut approaching. Cut to the juggernaut driving towards the corpse. Cut to* DAVINA, *mouth opening in a scream.*

INT. DANIEL'S HOUSE: BEDROOM. NIGHT
Cut to DANIEL *sitting up in bed, blinking. He puts his hands to his eyes as we hear slight noise over and see* SOPHIE, *snoring slightly, which is rather like the noise of a juggernaut approaching in the distance.*

INT. COURT CORRIDOR. DAY
STRAUSS, DANIEL, ZELDA *coming out of court, but we come straight in on* DANIEL *in his wig, looking slightly unfocused.*

STRAUSS: (*Out of shot*) Are you all right?

DANIEL: (*Blinks*) Yes, yes, just rather a bad night, thank you. Why?
(*Cut to* STRAUSS *stopping in the corridor.*)
STRAUSS: Well, I was just wondering if it was a ploy or you really did get his name wrong.
DANIEL: Whose?
STRAUSS: Detective Sergeant Cooper's.
(DANIEL *stares at him blankly, and we see beyond other people coming out of court, among them* COOKSON.)
ZELDA: (*Apologetically*) You kept calling him Detective Inspector Copper.
DANIEL: Merely a slip of the tongue.
STRAUSS: And Cropper. You also called him Cropper.
ZELDA: Some of the jury thought it was funny, anyway. Copper and Cropper for Cooper.
STRAUSS: (*Upset*) The judge didn't. There's Cookson, we better go and talk to him. Let him know our strategy. He looks a bit – um – concerned.
(*As* STRAUSS *speaks, an usher comes up to* DANIEL.)
USHER: Mr Davenport? Telephone.
DANIEL: (*To* STRAUSS) I'll be right back.
(*He hurries to the telephone, picks it up.*)
Hello, Davenport here.
(*Little pause.*)
QUASS: (*Voice over, telephone*) It's awful, Davenport. Awful.
DANIEL: Well, go on, tell me.
QUASS: (*Voice over, telephone*) I can't on the phone. It's a call box and I've only got one 10p and there's somebody else waiting.
DANIEL: Well, where are you then?
QUASS: (*Voice over, telephone*) A pub. The Rising Sun, Euston Road.
DANIEL: Euston Road! (*Looking at his watch*) All right. Stay there, I'll be right over.
(*He hangs up, comes out of the kiosk, makes to go, then sees* STRAUSS, ZELDA *and* COOKSON *staring at him.* DANIEL *goes over.*)
Look, something's come up. (*Hurrying to the door*) But don't worry, I'll be there in time to cook Cookson's goose.

STRAUSS: *Mr* Cookson is our client.

EXT. STREET NEAR LAWCOURT. DAY
DANIEL *trying to get a taxi, gown and wig over his arm. He carries them throughout the next sequence.*

EXT. THE RISING SUN. DAY
DANIEL *getting out of the taxi, entering the pub.*

INT. THE RISING SUN. DAY
It is crowded, as for lunchtime. QUASS *is not immediately visible.* DANIEL *stares around. The door to the gents opens.* QUASS's *head appears. He beckons to* DANIEL. DANIEL *goes to lavatory urinal, etc. It appears to be empty. Then* QUASS *opens the lavatory door.*

QUASS: In here.
    (DANIEL *goes to the entrance.*)

INT. THE RISING SUN: LAVATORY. DAY
QUASS *is sitting on the lavatory, seat down.*

DANIEL: What the hell are you doing?
QUASS: The smoke. Nearly killed me. The news is terrible,
    Davenport, terrible!
    (*And he fumbles sheets out of his pocket.*)
DANIEL: Yes, you've already told me that, get on with it. I've
    only got a few minutes.
    (*The sound of the door opening, footsteps.* DANIEL *closes the
    door, locks it. The following conversation is conducted in
    whispers.*)
    Well, go on, go on!
    (*He attempts to take the sheet from* QUASS's *hand.*)
QUASS: Coveney, Billington, Cropper, Wardle are in gaol. Just
    like Jackaboots.
DANIEL: Gaol!
QUASS: That's how your Mr Jackson found out so quickly.
    Phoned the school for their initials (*Talking slightly
    hysterically*) then phoned a friend of his on a newspaper just

on the offchance, and they all came up on the computer.
One after the other.

DANIEL: But – but what did they do?

QUASS: Billington tried to smuggle drugs into Turkey.
Cropper's doing five years for misappropriation. He was a
solicitor. Coveney and Wardle are doing five and three
years respectively. Wardle was party to a swindle connected
with a children's charity. Coveney was a hit-and-run case.
Wiped out a couple of pensioners and a social worker.
(*Cut to* DANIEL, *deeply disturbed.*)
And look – I've worked it out – the lines and blocks –
that's what the blocks mean. Gaol. And three lines for
Jackaboy on his way to gaol. A line for you on your way to
gaol. And Shulman – the crosses for me and Shulman –
(*Voice shaking*) are for death. Shulman flung himself under
a train at Archway tube station. So now we know why Mrs
Shulman sobbed when she hung up on you. Suicide
Shulman committed suicide. (*Whinnies with terrified
laughter.*) So either they drove him mad –

DANIEL: (*Dully*) Like Jackaboots.

QUASS: Or they pushed him under the train. And that's what
they've got in mind for me. Cross cross cross cross Quass.

DANIEL: (*Looks at watch.*) I've got to get back.
(*He turns towards the door. There is a terrible wheezing sound
from* QUASS. DANIEL *turns.* QUASS *clutches his chest,
collapses back, fumbles out his inhaler, drops it, is gasping so
much that he can't grope for it.* DANIEL, *momentarily torn
between leaving and helping, picks up spray.* QUASS's *arms are
hanging limp, his mouth agape. His wheeze is frightening.*
DANIEL *bends over him and squirts spray into his mouth.*
QUASS *recovers slowly. Cut from* QUASS's *face to* DANIEL's,
impatient.)
Are you all right?
(*He looks at him.* QUASS *nods, clearly enfeebled.*)
Can you get up?

QUASS: Yes, yes. You go. (*He gestures weakly.*)

DANIEL: (*Hesitates.*) Come on, I'll get you into a taxi.
(*He helps* QUASS *up. His wig is completely askew.* DANIEL

opens the door just as a MAN *passing, unzipping his flies, stares
in.* DANIEL *half supports* QUASS *out of lavatory.*)
QUASS: It's very kind of you, Davenport.
(*A couple of* OTHER MEN, *peeing, watch.*)

EXT. THE RISING SUN. DAY
It is now raining. Several occupied taxis go by, although DANIEL
*still gestures at them desperately. One comes along with the 'for hire'
sign on.* DANIEL *signals to it, all the time supporting* QUASS. *The*
TAXI DRIVER *slows down, sees* QUASS, *speeds off.*

DANIEL: What the – he must have thought you were drunk.
Can't you stand up properly, man? And put your – (*gestures
to his head*) – your – back.
(QUASS *adjusts his wig, tries to stand up. Another taxi
appears, stops.* DANIEL *helps* QUASS *into it.* QUASS *gets into it
shakily.*)
QUASS: (*As he does so, tremulously*) But what are we going to do?
DANIEL: (*Seeing another taxi approach*) I'll come round – I'll
come round this evening.
(*He shuts the door, signals to the taxi which goes on past him.
Cut to shot of* DANIEL *on pavement, shaking his fist at
retreating taxi, then shaking his wig and gown despairingly
towards another, occupied, taxi.*)

INT. CORRIDOR/COURT. DAY
The doors of the courtroom, seen from DANIEL's *point of view, as he
races towards them, struggling into his barrister's togs which are now
wet, his wig bedraggled, and take in from his point of view*
STRAUSS *turning, staring in suppressed anger, while* ZELDA *is rising
to her feet.* ZELDA *turns.* DANIEL, *advancing to the defence table,
takes the papers from her hand.*

DANIEL: Beg the court's um – sorry I'm late, m'lud. Um – may
I proceed with the witness? (*Going straight on*) Now,
Detector Inspective – Detective Inspector (*Then carefully*)
Cooper –
JUDGE: (*Out of shot, courteously*) Detective Inspector Cooper has
left the stand. This is Detective Inspector Sowerboy.

DANIEL: Indeed, m'lud.
(*He looks down at papers in his hand in evident bewilderment, then desperately fakes a cough.*)
Excuse me, m'lud, a touch of – a touch of – (*coughs slightly again*) – some water, please.
(*He turns to* ZELDA *and* STRAUSS.)

INT. COURT CORRIDOR. DAY
DANIEL, ZELDA, STRAUSS *walking along the corridor in silence.*

ZELDA: I thought you had him backing away at the end. (*To* STRAUSS) Didn't you?
STRAUSS: Yes. (*As they approach room*) Perhaps he thought the cough was contagious.
DANIEL: Look – I – I don't think I should speak any more this evening.
STRAUSS: You mean, not to Cookson?
DANIEL: Cookson?
STRAUSS: Our client!
DANIEL: Not to anyone.
STRAUSS: But he needs to hear your view.
DANIEL: Oh, for God's sake, Strauss, if a chap's losing his voice, he's losing his voice. Surely he'll understand that. Just tell him I can't speak, for God's sake! (*Bellowing*) My voice has gone, damn it!
(DANIEL *goes to the telephone booth. He picks up the telephone, dials.* SOPHIE, *voice over, answers, giving her telephone number.*)
How are you all?
SOPHIE: (*Voice over, telephone*) I've got a backy and cramps in the tum.
DANIEL: Oh, cramps, really? Well, the thing is, my lovey, to lie on the floor and lift your –
SOPHIE: (*Voice over, telephone*) Do you think it's started? Come home soon.
DANIEL: What? No, no, it can't be, not for another three weeks at least, eh? But, um, but that Greek I met last night –
SOPHIE: (*Voice over, telephone*) I thought he was Turkish.
DANIEL: Well, yes, Turk but resident in Greece, if you

remember. (*Pauses as if not quite sure he's got it right.*)
Anyway, Greek or Turk or whatever he is, Greek resident
in Turkey or Turkey resident in Greek –
(*He catches sight of* COOKSON, STRAUSS, *and* ZELDA *coming
down the corridor.* COOKSON, STRAUSS *and* ZELDA *approach
the telephone booth,* COOKSON *indignant. As they pass,*
DANIEL *is mouthing kisses down the telephone.*)

INT. QUASS'S HOUSE: LIVING ROOM. NIGHT
We come in on newspaper clippings spread out on the desk,
DANIEL's *hand pushing them around and we see from clipping to
clipping with headlines:* GRANTHAM SOLICITOR GAOLED;
KIDDIES' HEARTACHE AS CHARITY CON MAN GOES TO GAOL;
ARCHWAY STOCKBROKER INQUEST. WIFE DENIES SUICIDE;
ACCOUNTANT HELD IN TURKISH HELL-HOLE; *and then*
DARBY, JOAN, MISS DUTIFUL – MASSACRE AT THE
CROSSROADS.

DANIEL: (*Out of shot*) I can't tell anything from these. Just the
usual journalist's nonsense. 'Remained unmoved'; 'Broke
down and wept', etc.
QUASS: (*Out of shot*) But five boys out of one house from one
school. All gaoled over the last six months for different
offences. And Shulman's suicide.
DANIEL: (*Out of shot*) Yes.
(DANIEL *lays aside the newspaper cuttings, and helps himself
to a piece of fudge in the bowl beside him.*)
QUASS: (*Tentatively*) That Miss Wright in your message? Is that
something you could go to gaol for?
(DANIEL, *after a pause, nods.*)
DANIEL: The bit missing from your message. Is it something
you might commit suicide because of?
(QUASS, *after a pause, nods. There is a long pause. They stare
at each other.*)
QUASS: I tell, you tell. That was the agreement.
DANIEL: What did your message say, Nathaniel?
QUASS: It said. (*Draws breath.*) It said: 'Poor old Emmanuel.
Bowled out by Nathaniel.'
DANIEL: Who's Emmanuel?

QUASS: My brother. Older brother. Eleven years older.

DANIEL: What does it mean, 'bowled out by Nathaniel'?

QUASS: I bowled him out of the window. (*Points to french windows*) Killed him.

DANIEL: Why?

QUASS: He was trying to teach me the rules of cricket.

DANIEL: And that's why you killed him?

QUASS: Yes – no – I mean he was different from Nellie and me. Made himself into a perfect English type. Tall. Slim. Muscular. A head of hair. So, of course, he was accepted into the best public school. No mere Amplesides for him. One afternoon I was in here, scraping away at the violin, in he came, with a cricket bat. 'Now,' he said. 'Let me show you.' I said, 'Come on. Emmanuel, I'm practising violin, not cricket.' He said, 'It's time you bloody learnt the rules and the fundamentals of the game, at least.' 'I don't want to know about cricket,' I said. 'I'm happy with this.' Showing him my bow. He snatched it away from me and I tried to snatch it back and it went into his eye and suddenly there he was running backwards, skipping and jumping backwards, yowling, swinging his bat, right through the windows, over the porch, on to the terrace on to his head. It was an accident, Davenport.

DANIEL: Have you ever told anyone?

QUASS: I had a collapse. Nellie had to put me in hospital. I don't know what I said to the doctors, the other patients. (DANIEL *shakes his head.*)

DANIEL: (*Gently*) You're lying, Quass.

QUASS: What, you think I killed him on purpose?

DANIEL: No. I expect it was an accident all right. That's why it doesn't make sense. It's nothing for you to commit suicide for. After all these years. But you might commit suicide to protect Nellie.

(QUASS *bows his head.*)

QUASS: It happened just as I said. (*Little pause.*) He took away my bow. Nellie was just trying to get it back.

DANIEL: And that's what you might have told the doctors, the other patients? That Nellie killed him?

(QUASS *looks at him pathetically, nods. There is a pause.*)

QUASS: (*Tentatively*) So. So what about you, Davenport? No death in it, I hope?

DANIEL: Yes. Death in it.

QUASS: But you – you haven't killed anyone?

(DANIEL *puts another piece of fudge in his mouth abstractedly.*)

DANIEL: (*Slowly and painfully, chewing*) As a matter of fact, yes.

QUASS: (*After a little pause*) Miss Wright?

DANIEL: Her husband.

QUASS: You killed Miss Wright's husband?

DANIEL: She wasn't Miss Wright then. She was Mrs Hopjoy. Before that she was Miss Wright. Then later – after I killed her husband – she went back to being Miss Wright again. He was a university lecturer. He taught social sciences. No, social studies. One of those useless subjects –

(*He gestures. There is a pause.*)

QUASS: (*Waits.*) But that's not why you killed him? Because he taught a useless subject?

DANIEL: He was unbalanced, you see. Definitely unbalanced. When he somehow got wind that she and I were – he became very possessive. Very jealous.

QUASS: Well, isn't that, um, normal? With husbands. When their wives –

DANIEL: He wasn't her husband. Not when I came on the scene. Except in name. He'd left her a couple of years before. For one of his students. Several of his students as a matter of fact. But he still felt he had a claim on Davina. Used to follow her. And me. I have an idea he actually employed private detectives – anyway . . . (*Pause.*) He gave me no choice.

QUASS: (*Encouragingly*) How did you do it?

DANIEL: I – ran over him.

QUASS: (*Nods.*) Ran him over.

DANIEL: No, I didn't run him over. I ran over him. Quite different.

QUASS: Yes? In what respect?

DANIEL: One night I roared up to her door and felt this bump. A sort of soft bump. So I looked under the wheels. And there he was. He must've just laid himself out on the street

and – waited for me to go over him. It was suicide really.
But at my expense. Of course I should have gone to the
police. But then he was the husband, I was the lover,
Davina was the only witness, nobody would have believed
– although I don't know. I've discovered since then that
juries can be very perverse. I might have got one that
believed the truth. Especially with a good QC. Carstairs,
for instance. He was in his prime then. Before he took to
buying race horses – but still it would have ruined me, even
if I'd been acquitted. I'd certainly never have had the
slightest chance of ending up a judge.

QUASS: So that's what you want, is it?

DANIEL: Well, one day – it's possible – was possible.
(QUASS *nods.*)

QUASS: (*After a little pause*) What did you do?

DANIEL: Got his body into the car and drove it down to the
Mile End Road. Left it outside his college. Queen Mary
College. Lots of traffic, you see. Especially at dawn.
Apparently quite a lot of it went over him before anyone
noticed – so he was quite hard to identify. Took them
weeks.

QUASS: How long ago did this happen?

DANIEL: Nine years ago. Ten. Ten years ago. June 6th, 1979.

QUASS: Well, even if you were followed, they wouldn't wait ten
years, would they?

DANIEL: No, they wouldn't. It must be somebody who's found
out *now*. Look – let's look at the whole thing logically.
There must be a motive. What are the usual motives for
destroying people? Money? But they haven't asked for
money. Revenge?

QUASS: (*Breaking out suddenly*) But why death for me and
Shulman, and only gaol for you and Jackaboots? And the
rest. You know why. (*As if realizing*) I'll tell you why.
Because Shulman and I are Jewish. That's why! It's
discrimination.
(DANIEL *shakes his head.*)
How do you know?

DANIEL: Because I'm Jewish. And as they know everything else
about me, they're bound to know that, aren't they?

QUASS: (*Astonished*) You're Jewish?

    (DANIEL *nods.*)

    But I used to see you going into chapel every morning, to sing hymns, why, you even got confirmed, didn't you?

DANIEL: Yes. But it didn't mean anything. For some reason everyone assumed I was of C. of E. And of course I never quite got around to explaining – I just did what the others did.

QUASS: (*Muttering*) Well, one does have to conform. Or try to. As they say.

DANIEL: What?

QUASS: And are you still C. of E.?

DANIEL: No, of course not.

QUASS: Jewish again, then?

DANIEL: I regard myself first and foremost as a barrister.

QUASS: Well, shortly you may be regarding yourself as a gaolbird.

    (NELLIE *enters, carrying two letters and a bowl of toffee.*)

NELLIE: Here you are, one each, delivered by hand. Isn't that nice?

QUASS: (*Taking his letter*) Where – where did you get these?

NELLIE: From the mat, of course. I saw them lying on it when I was coming to give Daniel a refill. I knew he'd be ready for one. (*Putting down bowl*) This time, toffee, Daniel. Give your jaws something to work on. Well, go on, why don't you open them? Who are they from?

    (QUASS *and* DANIEL *open their letters.*)

QUASS: (*As he does so*) Oh, chaps from the old school that Davenport and I have asked to help in a little charity project. I'll tell you about it later, Nellie.

NELLIE: As long as it's not goat's cheeses and frozen turkeys to people who don't want them, eh, Daniel?

    (NELLIE *exits. There is a pause.*)

QUASS: What's – what's yours?

DANIEL: Mostly it's a signed statement from (*Looks at end*) Mavis and Donald Carper. (*Frowns as if a hint of memory at the name.*) Private investigators working on behalf of Geoffrey Hopjoy – (*His eye skimming through text*) – assigned to watch his wife, Davina Hopjoy's residence –

did witness the death of our client, Geoffrey Hopjoy, at one a.m. June 6th, 1979 – they say – they say I did it on purpose! Swerved on to the pavement – hit him – reversed over him – several times – (*Voice shaking*) – followed me to the forecourt of Queen Mary College, University of London – they've got – they say they've got photographs which they will send with a copy of this statement to the police, the bar association, every national newspaper, and to Mrs Davina Hopjoy *née* Wright, unless I comply with their instructions, which are *en route*. (*Looks up at* QUASS.) And yours?

QUASS: Signed statements from people at one of the – the homes I had to stay in. That I said that – that Nellie had killed Emmanuel. (*Looks at* DANIEL, *stricken*.) How could I, oh how could I – copies will be sent to Miss Nellie Quass to – (*Counting*) – every rabbi in London, and the Chief Rabbi of Leeds – why Leeds? And the police of course. Unless I comply with their instructions which are *en route*.
(*They stare at each other.*)
Instructions for what? Instructions to me to commit suicide? Instructions to you to get yourself sent to gaol? What can they want, Davenport?
(*Doorbell rings.* QUASS *and* DANIEL *look at each other.* QUASS *gets up, goes over to the window, looks down.* DANIEL *joins him. We see from* QUASS's *and* DANIEL's *point of view a* MESSENGER *in helmet, goggles and gauntlets, holding two envelopes. The door opens. The* MESSENGER *hands over the two envelopes and a board with pencil. The board is handed back. The* MESSENGER *continues to stand there with the board.*)
What's going on? What's she doing? Why's he still there?
(*The* MESSENGER *takes off a gauntlet, bends forward towards the doorway, takes something between his fingers, puts it in his mouth, nods, turns. We see from* DANIEL's *point of view the* MESSENGER *stopping for a moment, putting his finger in his mouth, trying to fish something out with his finger, gives up. The* MESSENGER *goes around the corner. Sound of motorbike over the sound of* NELLIE *coming upstairs.*)
NELLIE: (*Out of shot*) Two more! One for each of you. (*Enters.*)

Oh, look at you, such friends you've become all over again.
(*Gives them an envelope each.*) After these years – too many
years you don't see each other – what I want is you bring
your wife and twins around, Daniel, all of us together –
(*She is becoming emotional, turns, goes out hurriedly.* DANIEL
and QUASS *rip open their envelopes.* QUASS *stares at* DANIEL
radiantly.)

QUASS: Money. Only money they want. And so little. (*Claps his
hands.*) Who would have believed it!

DANIEL: How much?

QUASS: Twenty thousand, that's all. And you?

DANIEL: (*Ashen, not sharing* QUASS's *jubilation*) Twenty-five
thousand. (*Repeats.*) Twenty-five thousand. (*Reading*) The
monies will be in denominations of five-pound notes. We
will take delivery at the gate to platform ten, Waterloo
Station, at one p.m. tomorrow. You will carry for both
parties. There will be a telephone call immediately after
receipt of this communication with further details.

QUASS: (*Reads:*) You will accompany the carrier to Waterloo
Station and then wait at the gate of platform nine until the
transaction is completed.
(DANIEL *puts a toffee into his mouth.*)
Once you have begun the journey to Waterloo Station you
will not make any contact with the monies. You will also
control your wheezing and so avoid making a public
spectacle of yourself. There will be a telephone call
immediately on receipt of this communication giving
further details.
(*The telephone rings.* QUASS *reaches for telephone, goes on
reading,* CARPER *is on the other end.*)
Which your accomplice must answer.
(QUASS *hands the telephone to* DANIEL.)
Answer it, Davenport, answer it.
(DANIEL, *struggling desperately with the toffee in his mouth,
makes gagging noises down the telephone of 'Yes', 'I
understand', and 'Right'.* QUASS *snatches the telephone from
him.*)
(*Babblingly*) I'm sorry for my friend, his mouth is full of
toffee.

(DANIEL, *swallowing the toffee, snatches the telephone back.*)

DANIEL: Hello, yes. (*Listens.*) Yes, yes, I've got all that, but listen – please – (*listens*) – you've already said all that, a man in a green cap, yes, but how – (*listens*) yes, I've got it – (*Looks at* QUASS.) He keeps repeating the same thing.

QUASS: It must be a recording.

DANIEL: Oh. (*Listens again as the voice goes metallically on.*) Yes – (*He puts the telephone down.*)

QUASS: What did he say?

DANIEL: (*Listlessly*) That a man in a green cap would be waiting at the gate to the platform. I'm to identify myself by saying, 'I'm carrying the agreed sum. Here it is.' Then I give it to him and say, 'Thank you. Goodbye.' So – so just common criminals after all. We ought to go – (*tries to draw himself up*) – we have a duty to go. To the police.

QUASS: The police! (*Squawking*) The police – when they've got this – (*Shaking his statements*) – if anything happened to Nellie – they're right. I'd – I'd kill myself.

DANIEL: But they're just blackmailers and everybody knows blackmailers never stop after the first payment. In fact it encourages them to go on. I defended a chap once. An absolute swine. He blackmailed illegal immigrants. Charged them *weekly*. That's the way they operate.

QUASS: What happened to him?

DANIEL: Oh. I got him off.

QUASS: And the illegal immigrants. What happened to them?

DANIEL: They got sent back to – (*Remembers where they got sent back to*) – a country recognized by Her Majesty's Government. (*Slams his hand down on the desk.*) For God's sake, Quass, what does it matter what happened to them, what matters is, what matters is – (*Swelling, then subsiding*) – what matters is I haven't got twenty-five thousand pounds. Not available in cash, anyway.

QUASS: (*Disbelieving*) But surely you could raise it?

DANIEL: Not easily. I've got commitments – the mortgage, heavy insurance. And the car, of course. That bloody car. Why did I ever allow myself? Bootsie warned me. But everything was beginning to go so well. More and more cases. Getting quite a reputation at last. (*Stops.*) Of course,

if they give me time, three weeks, a month. (*Pause. Gets up.*) I'd better go. I've got to be in court tomorrow. Possibly for the last time, eh? Or rather the last time in a professional capacity. The next time I suppose I'll be in the dock. And now I must go home to my wife. (*Looks at* QUASS.) Good luck for tomorrow. I'll be – be very pleased for you if it's the end of it. My best to Nellie.
(*He turns, goes out.* QUASS *sits for a moment, then gets up, hurries out. We see* DANIEL *just about to go out through the door.*)

QUASS: Wait – wait a minute, Davenport!
(*He hurries down.*)

EXT. QUASS'S HOUSE. NIGHT
DANIEL, *who has stepped outside, turns.* QUASS *closes the door behind him.*

QUASS: (*In a low voice*) You're giving up? Just because you haven't got the money?

DANIEL: What else can I do if I haven't got the money? By tomorrow, remember, one p.m.

QUASS: Ssssh. (*Points to entry phone.*) You could ask me.

DANIEL: (*Relief visible*) But I – I might not be able to repay it for years.

QUASS: Repay when you can. If you can't, don't.
(DANIEL *makes to speak emotionally. Checks himself.*)

DANIEL: (*Formally*) It's really very good of you, Quass.

QUASS: No, it's not. It's easy. Easy isn't good. Simply easy.

DANIEL: (*Smiling*) That sounded – sounded extremely like Nellie.

QUASS: Then I was at my best. Money I can afford. More of this – (*Putting his hand to chest, shakes his head.*) So no more about the money except what we've got to do tomorrow. I'll go to the bank and draw out forty-five thousand pounds in cash –
(DANIEL *flinches slightly.*)
– and then meet you. Where do I meet you?

DANIEL: I've got to be in court until twelve thirty. Old Bailey.

Court number five. We should just do it from there to
Waterloo.

QUASS: I'll come in a hired car. We'll go straight on –

DANIEL: No, by tube. The traffic at lunchtime – we're much
safer by tube. Don't forget to take a bag – a big one –

QUASS: Two. I'll take two. Forty-five thousand in fivers –

NELLIE: (*Voice over, entry phone*) Is that you two whispering
away down there?

QUASS: Just saying good night, Nellie.

NELLIE: (*Voice over, entry phone*) What about a good night to
me, shame to you, Daniel.

DANIEL: Sorry, Nellie. Good night.

(*They shake hands.*)

QUASS: (*Solemnly*) Tomorrow then.

DANIEL: Tomorrow then. And – thank you, Nathaniel.

EXT. DANIEL'S HOUSE. NIGHT

DANIEL *arriving in front of his house. One light on in the sitting
room. He opens the front door.*

INT. DANIEL'S HOUSE: HALL. NIGHT

Slightly eerie sensation. DANIEL *composes himself, goes upstairs,
opens sitting-room door.*

INT. DANIEL'S HOUSE: SITTING ROOM. NIGHT

*The television is on. There are signs of recent lolling on the sofa, but
the room is empty.* DANIEL *sees the study door half open, light on.
He goes in.*

INT. DANIEL'S HOUSE: STUDY. NIGHT

DANIEL: Bootsie?

(*It is empty. He sees one message on the machine. He turns,
goes out, goes on up to the bedroom.*)

INT. DANIEL'S HOUSE: BEDROOM. NIGHT

Clothes spilled across the floor. Bed unmade. DANIEL, *clearly
getting anxious, goes to bathroom. It is empty.*

INT. DANIEL'S HOUSE. NIGHT
Montage:
DANIEL *opening door on twins' room.*
Calling, 'Bootsie! Bootsie!' with increasing desperation as he goes on to kitchen, laundry room.
He goes back to the sitting room, panic-stricken.
Enters the study again.

INT. DANIEL'S HOUSE: STUDY. NIGHT
DANIEL *sees the telephone answering machine, is about to go out, then stops, turns, plays the message.*

SOPHIE: (*On machine, pathetically*) Oh, Popsie, I didn't know where to get hold of you. You didn't even leave a number. I've tried everywhere, and now they're coming to get me and you won't even be there to help –
(*The message is obviously continuing, but:*)

INT. HOSPITAL CORRIDOR. NIGHT
DANIEL, *hurrying down hospital corridor to maternity-ward desk. A* NURSE *or whatever is sitting at it, crisp-looking, efficient.*

DANIEL: Mrs Davenport, please. I'm her husband.
(*He is breathless, sweating.*)
NURSE: (*Looking down list*) Ah, yes. (*Smiles.*) Congratulations, Mr Davenport. You're the father of an eight-pound six-ounce girl.
DANIEL: Only one. (*Still fighting for breath*) But there are meant to be two. (*Little pause.*) Twins.
(*The* NURSE *frowns, looks at the list again.*)
NURSE: Well, only one's been delivered. So far, anyway.

INT. HOSPITAL CORRIDOR. NIGHT
Cut to DANIEL *and* NURSE *going down another corridor. They stop before a door. The* NURSE *is about to push the door open.* DANIEL *sees, through window, a baby in a cot.*

DANIEL: That's not mine.
(*The* NURSE *looks at him.*)

NURSE: How do you know?

DANIEL: Because – because – (*Gestures towards the woman in the bed*) – that's not my wife.

(*The* NURSE *looks at her list.*)

NURSE: (*Firmly*) Dandidop. D–6.

DANIEL: No, Davenport. Davenport.

INT. HOSPITAL CORRIDOR. NIGHT
DANIEL *and the* NURSE *hurrying down another corridor, stopping before a private room.* DANIEL *goes in.*

INT. HOSPITAL PRIVATE ROOM. NIGHT
SOPHIE: (*Seeing* DANIEL) Oh, Popsie, Popsie, where have you been?

(*He goes to her, takes her hand, kisses her.*)

DANIEL: The important thing is I'm here in time. (*Moved*) Oh, my Bootsie!

(*He kisses her on the forehead.*)

INT. HOSPITAL PRIVATE ROOM. NIGHT
Montage:
SOPHIE *in mild labour,* DANIEL *sitting beside her.*
SOPHIE *sleeping seraphically,* DANIEL *in chair,* SOPHIE *in mild labour,* DANIEL *staring anxiously,* SOPHIE *asleep again,* SOPHIE *in labour, then shot after shot of* SOPHIE *at seemingly the same stage of labour.*

INT. HOSPITAL PRIVATE ROOM. DAY
Later. We come in on DANIEL *asleep on a chair by the bed, snoring slightly. The bed is empty. A* DOCTOR *enters, comes over, shakes* DANIEL's *arm.* DANIEL *lurches into consciousness, stares up, clearly unaware of where he is.*

DOCTOR: They're on their way, Mr Davenport. They'll be here any minute.

DANIEL: Who?

INT. HOSPITAL CORRIDOR. DAY
As they walk along the corridor:

DOCTOR: Your wife's in tip-top form – well, considering she's
   been at it for fourteen hours or so.
DANIEL: What, fourteen – !
   (*He looks at his watch. Cut to watch: it is twelve ten.*)
   (*Staring in panic at the* DOCTOR) Oh, my God – I've got to
   go.
DOCTOR: But your babies will be here –
DANIEL: No, no. (*Beginning to run off*) I've got to be somewhere
   important by twelve thirty. Matter of life and –
   (*He jogs off along hospital corridor.*)

INT. COURT CORRIDOR. DAY
DANIEL *is jogging desperately along the court corridor, various
solicitors, barristers, clients conferring, among them* COOKSON,
ZELDA *and* STRAUSS, *all obviously worried. They see* DANIEL
coming. STRAUSS *comes towards* DANIEL.

STRAUSS: (*In an angry whisper*) Where the hell have you been?
   Zelda's been making a dreadful hash of the cross-
   examination –
   (DANIEL, *not listening, spots* QUASS *looking absolutely frantic,
   tapping his watch, two enormous overnight bags in front of
   him.*)
DANIEL: (*To* STRAUSS) It's Sophie – she's having the babies –
   I've got to get back to the hospital – come on, man, come
   on –
   (*He gestures to* QUASS. QUASS *hurries over.* DANIEL *takes*
   QUASS's *arm.*)
QUASS: Where have you been?
DANIEL: (*For* STRAUSS's *benefit*) We've got to get to the
   hospital –
QUASS: Hospital! Waterloo. We've got to get to Waterloo.
   What's the matter with you –
   (STRAUSS *hears this.* DANIEL *pulls* QUASS *away, and we see
   them, from* STRAUSS's *point of view jogging along the corridor.*
   COOKSON *has come over to him.*)

COOKSON: I haven't got a chance, have I? (*Bitterly, gazing after retreating* QUASS *and* DANIEL) I'm going to do that bastard. When I get out.

EXT. WATERLOO UNDERGROUND: STAIRS TO MAIN STATION. DAY
DANIEL *and* QUASS *struggling up the stairs with other passengers.*

QUASS: What are you going to call them?
(DANIEL *looks at his watch.*)
DANIEL: Seven minutes to. Should have gone by taxi – never trust London Transport. Never.
QUASS: What a pity – what a pity you missed the birth, eh?
DANIEL: (*Stops suddenly.*) Give me the bags!
QUASS: What?
DANIEL: Give me the bags! I'm meant to be carrying them, remember!
QUASS: Oh – oh God, yes!
(*He pushes them at* DANIEL, *begins to wheeze, fumbling in his pocket.*)
DANIEL: Oh no, not now. Please not now!
QUASS: Just – just one second. They said I'm not to wheeze –
(*He has taken out his inhaler, is trying to break the seal.*
DANIEL *takes it from him, breaks the seal, hands the inhaler back to* QUASS.)
(*Squirts*) There. There. Right – right, Davenport.
(*They move off,* DANIEL *surging ahead with bags,* QUASS *shakily labouring after him.*)

INT. WATERLOO STATION. DAY
DANIEL *and* QUASS. *We see the clock from their point of view. It is six minutes to one. Cut to* QUASS, *staring at* DANIEL, *his expression one of dreadful tension as he tries to control his wheezing.* DANIEL *hesitates, suddenly reaches out his hand, squeezes* QUASS's *arm.* DANIEL *turns away, and we see him from* QUASS's *point of view walking to platform ten, then cut to* DANIEL's *point of view, eyes flicking around as he stands with his bag, clocking various faces. We see them from his point of view and also* QUASS *watching, from* DANIEL's *point of view and then cut to* QUASS, *and we see from his*

point of view DANIEL *waiting. He takes in a number of* MEN, *one seen by him, not by* DANIEL, *and then* TWO MEN *together.* DANIEL *looking at the* TWO MEN, *then looking past them, then we see, also from* QUASS's *point of view,* CARPER *talking to the* CAMERA LADY *and* PARKES. CARPER *takes a green cap out of his pocket, pulls it low over his eyes, begins to edge towards* DANIEL. QUASS *begins to wheeze and reaches for his inhaler. Cut to* DANIEL, *and we see from his point of view* QUASS *about to use his inhaler.* QUASS *is suddenly jostled and the inhaler falls from his hand.* QUASS *tries to pick it up, is jostled again by* LARGE MAN, *(camera lady's companion), then falls. All this seen from* DANIEL's *point of view. We see* MAN *picking up the inhaler, then helping* QUASS *to his feet, dusting him down. There is something odd in the whole sequence. Then* DANIEL *spots Carper's green cap pulled very low, partly but not properly recognizes* CARPER, *who is moving towards him. Then* DANIEL *sees, loitering some way behind* CARPER, PARKES, *then the* CAMERA WOMAN. CARPER *comes up to* DANIEL, *his face lowered.* DANIEL *stares at him, says nothing.*

CARPER: (*Head still down*) There's something you're meant to say to me. (*Pause.*) Shall I take these, Mr Davenport? (*He reaches for the bags.*)

DANIEL: Don't touch them! If you don't stop molesting me, I shall call a policeman.
(CARPER *lifts his head, stares at him. We see* CARPER *full face.* DANIEL *turns, hurries over to* QUASS.)
Come on, come on, we've got to get away. It's a trap. There are people all around –
(*He shoves a bag into* QUASS's *hand, takes his arm, strides off.* QUASS *stumbles beside him, breathing heavily.*)
Keep walking!

INT. TAXI. DAY
QUASS *slumped in a corner,* DANIEL *sitting tensely.*

QUASS: (*Wheezing slightly*) Who – who were they?

DANIEL: The one in the green cap – the other day he gave me some information about the other one – and asked for twenty-five thousand pounds. I thought it was a joke – I

suppose the others were police. And the woman with a
camera – a reporter, I suppose. So police and press. That's
who they were. If I'd handed over the money – (*Gestures.*)
My God! A barrister! Bribing a witness! That's the sort of
thing *solicitors* do! But a barrister! Never! Do you realize
what it means? The sheer cold *planning* that's gone into it –
just to get me into gaol! Such lengths – such lengths! I
wonder what they'd planned for you. Push you under a
train? I saw that man, the one who knocked you over. He
was up to something.
(*He looks at* QUASS, *sees him properly.* QUASS *is lying back
helpless, struggling for breath, feebly groping in his pocket for
his inhaler. His condition is clearly desperate.* DANIEL, *in a
panic, reaches over, fumbles in Quass's pocket, pulls out the
inhaler, turns to* QUASS, *who is lying back, mouth agape,
fighting for breath.* DANIEL *makes to apply the inhaler, then
snatches it away in horror, looks at it.*)
But this one's got a cap! That man trod on it at Waterloo. I
saw. This isn't the same one. He must have substituted it.
(QUASS, *unable to reply, sits fighting for breath, his hand
flapping loosely towards the inhaler, then letting it flap back.*
DANIEL *leans forward.*)
(*To* TAXI DRIVER) Hurry, please hurry!

INT. QUASS'S HOUSE: HALL. DAY
NELLIE *and* DANIEL *dragging* QUASS *along.*

NELLIE: Oh, look at him – look at him – I warned him – why
didn't he use his spray? Why?
DANIEL: There was something wrong with it.
NELLIE: With both of them, impossible!
DANIEL: (*Panting*) Both of them?
NELLIE: I always put two in his pocket, in case. Two fresh
ones. Every morning.
(*Cut to* DANIEL's *face, appalled.*)
(*Out of shot*) In here – get him in here –
(*She is drawing them to a door that hasn't been opened before.*)
(*To* QUASS, *crooningly*) Oh, my *Liebchen, hier, mein
Liebchen, Nellie ist mit dir, Nell ist mit dir* –

INT. QUASS'S HOUSE: SICKROOM. DAY
They struggle into a large room with a bed in it, an oxygen tent, all sorts of medical equipment, in fact a small emergency ward. There is a trestle.

NELLIE: (*As they get* QUASS *on to the bed*) Get his clothes off.
(DANIEL *begins to undress* QUASS *awkwardly.* QUASS *is now unconscious, in a coma.*)
DANIEL: Surely – surely what he needs – (*As he continues the undressing*) – is to be able to breathe?
NELLIE: I know what he needs.
(DANIEL *is in a panic, which he attempts to control.*)
DANIEL: He's going, Nellie. Going.
NELLIE: Be quiet, be quick!
(*She comes back with an oxygen mask, which she clamps over* QUASS'S *mouth.* DANIEL *has now got* QUASS *down to his underpants.*)
(*Indicating oxygen mask*) Here. Hold this.
(DANIEL *takes the mask as* NELLIE *peels down* QUASS'S *underpants speedily, goes to the trestle. Cut between* QUASS'S *face, with the mask over it;* DANIEL'S *face, intent;* NELLIE *bustlingly arranging the trestle.*)
Now. (*Coming back*) Let's bring him over.
(*They lift* QUASS *with difficulty over to the trestle,* DANIEL *just managing to keep the mask on, though it slips once or twice. They arrange him face forward over the trestle.* NELLIE *attaches the mask securely, with a strap.* NELLIE *goes to a shelf, opens a bottle.*)
Here. Rub this in with your hand.
DANIEL: Where?
NELLIE: Everywhere. Touch him, stroke him, soothe him – that's what he needs. Your body's warmth. Your body's tenderness. Your body's love. Give him your love through your fingers. Everywhere, Davenport.
(DANIEL *opens the bottle, rubs the ointment on* QUASS'S *back, shoulders.* NELLIE *goes to the hi-fi set, sorts out a tape, puts it on: Mozart. It fills the room.*)
This also he needs. So – rub underneath – around – every little patch, reach it with your love and care, Daniel.

(DANIEL *continues to rub, intensely.* NELLIE *comes over to him.*)
Now I'll do the rest. (*Takes the bottle from* DANIEL.) Thank you, Daniel. Now you go. Wait outside.
(*She begins to rub the ointment into* QUASS. *As she does so, she croons to the music.* DANIEL *goes to the door, turns; we see from his point of view* NELLIE *rubbing, crooning. She turns to him. Her eyes are full of panic. Then she goes back to crooning, her voice as if inspired.*)

INT. QUASS'S HOUSE: HALL. DAY
DANIEL *closes the door. Clearly deeply exhausted, he stands, then turns, goes almost automatically into the study.*

INT. QUASS'S HOUSE: STUDY. DAY
DANIEL *hesitates, looks around, sees a cupboard. Through this, faintly, the sound of* NELLIE *singing to Mozart.* DANIEL *goes to the cupboard, finds bottles of alcohol, takes out a bottle of whisky, looks around for a glass, can't see one, takes a swig from the bottle. Rocks slightly. Puts the bottle down, then picks it up again, takes a small gulp. Mozart and* NELLIE, *over, stop.* DANIEL *rubs his eyes, yawns, takes another gulp. As he lowers the bottle, he stops, listening. Slight noises off of a door opening. Low voices. Footsteps. He puts down the bottle and goes to the door, looks down the corridor and we see from his point of view.*

INT. QUASS'S HOUSE: HALL. DAY
The CAMERA WOMAN (*but without camera*) *coming out of a room down the hall, followed by* PARKES *and* CARPER *and her* COMPANION *from the wine bar. As they approach the sickroom, that door opens as if they have been summoned. They file in. The door closes.* DANIEL *blinks, dazed. He goes to the sickroom, stands for a moment, then sees that the door of the room from which the* CAMERA WOMAN, CARPER *and* PARKES *and the* COMPANION *have come is open. He goes to it.*

INT. QUASS'S HOUSE: BUGGING CENTRE. DAY
It is a highly sophisticated bugging centre for the house. There is a television screen, on which is a picture of the room that DANIEL *has*

*just left, the bottle of whisky in evidence. On the table in the
bugging centre, a board of buttons with labels for each button:*
STUDY, DINING ROOM, STAIRS, LIVING ROOM, FRONT HALL,
etc., and a button marked VIDEO. *On another table there are mugs
of half-drunk tea, a bottle of whisky and some glasses, gauntlets and
helmet and* CARPER's *green cap.* DANIEL *stares around him, then
presses a button marked* STUDY. *We see Quass's study on the screen.
Then he presses the button marked* FRONT HALL, *then stabs his
finger randomly down on each button in quick succession so we see
shots of different parts of the house on the screen. The last button he
presses is* VIDEO. DANIEL *and* QUASS *appear on the screen.*

QUASS: (*On screen*) So. So what about you, Davenport? No
    death in it, I hope?
DANIEL: (*On screen*) Yes. Death in it.
QUASS: (*On screen*) But you – you haven't killed anyone?
    (DANIEL *on the screen. He puts a piece of fudge into his
    mouth.*)
DANIEL: (*Chewing*) As a matter of fact, yes.
    (*Cut to* DANIEL's *finger stabbing down the button. The screen
    goes blank. He turns, looks around wildly, sees a stack of files
    on a shelf, then spots one on the desk under the shelf marked
    *JACKABOY.J. *He opens it. There is a caricature of* JACKABOY,
    *doing a nazi salute as he marches unheedingly towards an open
    manhole. He flicks on, a few photographs of* JACKABOY *at
    school, receiving his degree, etc. Then a small clipping:*
    'PROMINENT GYNAECOLOGIST EXONERATED', *then a
    series of papers, marked* CONFIDENTIAL: *hospital reports on
    the competence of* JACKABOY. DANIEL *looks up, takes in a
    row of files on the shelf marked* DAVENPORT. D. 1965–1975
    and DAVENPORT. D. 1976–1989. *He plucks the one down
    marked* 1965–1975, *opens it. We see from* DANIEL's *point of
    view photographs from Amplesides' house yearbook: shots of*
    DANIEL *playing cricket, receiving an award, etc. Cut to*
    DANIEL. *He puts the file back, seizes the other one. Cut to
    picture of* DAVINA *and* DANIEL *walking in the park, holding
    hands. Then newspaper cuttings, small, with such headlines as:*
    MYSTERY DEATH OF UNIVERSITY DON, *and* MILE END
    HORROR ACCIDENT, *and* RUN OVER – AT LEAST TWELVE

TIMES! *with photographs of Queen Mary College, and, on the first one, a photograph of a man in his mid thirties, bespectacled; under it* DOCTOR GEOFFREY HOPJOY. *Then a number of photographs, one of which is* DANIEL *laying the corpse on Mile End Road, and a recent one of* DANIEL *walking with* SOPHIE, *then one of the birthday dinner at Luigi's,* DANIEL *blowing out the candles on the cake,* SOPHIE *smiling and pregnant. As* DANIEL *looks at the last photograph, file in hand, the door opens.* NELLIE *enters.*)

NELLIE: Would you like to come and see him, Daniel? He's ready for you.

DANIEL: (*Almost as if he hasn't heard*) You've been following me, watching me all these years? Years and years?

NELLIE: Oh. (*Looks around.*) Yes, that's right, Daniel.

DANIEL: And those people – Parkes and that other one. Committing bribery, perjury. They're just your hirelings.

NELLIE: Oh, no. They're our *friends*, Daniel – Sidney, Donald, Mavis and Harold. Part of the team.

DANIEL: All this – all this just to ruin my life?

NELLIE: Ruin? Is your life ruined? I don't see ruin, Daniel, I see unshaven, bewildered, and I smell – um, well, not surprising, no change of clothes for two days. But ruin – do you think Nathaniel could *ruin* anyone, anything?

DANIEL: (*After a small pause*) He ruined all the others. Got them into gaol. Had one of them killed.

NELLIE: Just cases we found in the papers. The right age to have been with you at Amplesides is all. What, run over old-age pensioners and a social worker? The idea!

DANIEL: But Jackaboots. Boy. I saw with my own eyes what you did to him.

NELLIE: Oh, we didn't do much. Little things. Stole his trousers. Imitated the police now and then. The rest he did to himself. We never meant for him to go mad with knives and such. Just a little breakdown, we hoped. To convince you, you see, Daniel.

DANIEL: Are you saying that everything – everything you did – (*Gestures around room*) – was really because of me?

NELLIE: Because of you, Daniel, yes.

DANIEL: Why, Nellie? Why?

NELLIE: You still don't remember?
(DANIEL *shakes his head.*)
One afternoon he's in the music room, pouring himself out
through his violin. When the door bursts open and in come
some boys. Well-fed English chaps, with beaming faces,
and drag him off to the locker room and stuff him into a
locker and lock it.

DANIEL: Not me, Nellie. Not me. I couldn't do such a thing.
Even at Amplesides.

NELLIE: Then you and Jackaboots come in and hear him
crying. And Jackaboots unlocks the locker and laughs and
you, Daniel, the older brother he never had, look down on
Nathaniel and you smile. And then you wink. A lovely look
and smile and wink, perfect Church of English, and you
say – you say – (*Little pause.*)

DANIEL: Oh dear, well one does have to conform . . . (*After a
long pause*) But that was twenty-five years ago, Nellie.
Twenty-five years.

NELLIE: Twenty-five years of heart trouble, asthma, steroids,
hair falling out – twenty-five years of never to be a
musician, never to play in public, and now dead. (*Gently*)
That's a ruined life, Daniel.

DANIEL: (*Swaying slightly*) So I see it was revenge after all.

NELLIE: Revenge! Oh, that must be the way I told it, Daniel.
Don't think revenge. Think instead Nathaniel. Think love.
Hope. Fun and games. With a touch of revenge mixed in.
Like pepper. To add salt. There. Now you have it.
Anyway, it's finished, Daniel. All over. So come and say
your goodbyes to Nathaniel.
(*She turns, goes out of the door.* DANIEL *follows her,
will-less.*)

INT. QUASS'S HOUSE: HALL/STAIRS. DAY
NELLIE *leads him past the room* QUASS *was in, to the living room.
She opens the door.*

INT. QUASS'S HOUSE: LIVING ROOM. DAY
We come in on QUASS *dead, his body arranged in a hard-backed
chair. He is wearing a very smart, well-tailored dinner-jacket. He is*

gripping his violin and bow. The bow is resting against the strings of his violin. His eyes are open. His mouth is set in a slight smile. DANIEL stands, mesmerized. QUASS's bow twitches. A slight sound from the violin. The bow twitches again. Pause. Twitches again. Pause. Twitches again. Each time a sound from the violin. Then twitch again, but go on from twitch into playing, but mechanically, as if QUASS were a doll. The piece is the piece that he choked on earlier, when playing to NELLIE and DANIEL. As QUASS continues to play, he becomes less and less wooden, though his expression remains as in death. When he is playing dexterously, fluently, he rises from the chair. Flickers of life begin to appear on QUASS's face, transforming it by fleeting stages into one of delighted concentration, the music soaring past the point at which he abandoned it previously. QUASS's wig begins to slip a little, as he plays feverishly. Then hold on him for the finale. At the conclusion, the music still trembling in the air, he stops. He is drenched with sweat. He steps forward, shaking, takes a little bow. There is a pause.

DANIEL: Thank you.

INT. QUASS'S HOUSE: LIVING ROOM/MATERNITY ROOM. DAY *DANIEL turns, looks at NELLIE, goes to the door, opens it, and we see from his point of view as if the door has opened directly on to the maternity room, SOPHIE in bed, a baby in each arm. She smiles from one to the other and then towards DANIEL. He closes the door behind him, steps forward, goes over to the bed and we move back to take in the Davenport family as a group.*

A Month in the Country

A Month in the Country was first shown at the Warner West End Cinema in November 1987.
The cast was as follows:

BIRKIN	Colin Firth
MOON	Kenneth Branagh
MRS KEACH	Natasha Richardson
REVEREND KEACH	Patrick Malahide
DOUTHWAITE	Tony Haygarth
ELLERBECK	Jim Carter
COLONEL HEBRON	Richard Vernon
Director of Photography	Ken MacMillan
Production Designer	Leo Austin
Costumes	Judy Moorcroft
Editor	John Victor Smith
Producer	Kenith Trodd
Director	Pat O'Connor

A Pennies From Heaven Production.

ACT ONE

EXT. NO MAN'S LAND. DAY
A wasteland of mud. Rain. A SOLDIER *lies huddled alone, transmitter by his side, hands clamped around his head. The terrible sounds of war pushing him into the slime. We track slowly in to* BIRKIN.

INT. LONDON BEDROOM. NIGHT
BIRKIN's *face in the middle of a nightmare. Suddenly he wakes up with a howl, sits up in bed sweating, twitching.*

BIRKIN: V–, Vi–, Vinny, Vinny.

INT. TRAIN COMPARTMENT. DAY
BIRKIN *among Southerners. Cut to* BIRKIN's *face. His cheek begins to twitch uncontrollably. He takes out of his pocket a packet of ten Woodbine, opens it. There are five inside. Takes one out, lights it. His hand is trembling slightly. Sits smoking as twitch subsides. Becomes aware of man in corner, watching him. Puts his hand up over his twitch, sits smoking.*

EXT. LOCAL STATION, NORTH COUNTRY. DAY
Overcast. BIRKIN *on the platform by himself at one end with baggage. A few other people gathered at the other end. Beside him the local train clatters up.*

INT. TRAIN COMPARTMENT. DAY
BIRKIN *sitting in corner. We see from his point of view other faces in the compartment, all of them dour. An old man by the window staring at him with what seems like hostility. Rain sliding down the window beside him.* BIRKIN *takes out a cigarette packet. A half-cigarette left, he takes it out, looks at it, is about to light it when the train stops. He hears over a voice shouting what could be 'Oxgodby'. He peers through the window and just distinguishes the sign* OXGODBY. BIRKIN, *putting the cigarette back in the packet, gets*

71

up, struggles out on to the platform with his kitbag, etc., eliciting a few grunts as he treads on toes, seeming almost deliberately.

EXT. LOCAL STATION PLATFORM. DAY
Rain. BIRKIN *shuts the door, taking a last look at the dour faces as he does so. He is about to turn away. The* OLD MAN *in the compartment raps on the window, opens it.*

OLD MAN: Thoo's ga-ing ti git rare an' soaked reet down ti skin, maister.
(*Cut to* BIRKIN'*s face staring at him uncomprehendingly. Then he turns. He trudges down the platform in the rain. Cut to a girl of twelve, standing watching him from the station-house window.*)
ELLERBECK: (*Stationmaster*) Ticket, please.
(BIRKIN *fumbles for ticket, gives it to him.*)
(*Grimly*) Too can borrah me ombrella if that wantst.
(*It's almost incomprehensible.* BIRKIN *twitches slightly.*)
BIRKIN: What?
ELLERBECK: (*Enunciating carefully*) I said you can borrow my umbrella.
BIRKIN: Th–thank you. But I'm not g–g–g– (*Stops. Then, making an effort*) Going far.
ELLERBECK: A cup of tea then. In station house.
(ELLERBECK *nods towards station house, and we take in the girl –* KATHY *– still watching from window, now joined by a small boy –* EDGAR.)
BIRKIN: Th–th–th–thank you. But I have an appointment.
ELLERBECK: Aye. (*Nods.*) I know, you've come to the church, haven't you?
(BIRKIN *looks at him, nods.*)
(*Out of shot, shouting*) Well, if you don't find what you're looking for there, come see us other lot up at chapel.
BIRKIN: Th – thank you.
(ELLERBECK *nods at* BIRKIN. BIRKIN *turns, goes on.*)
ELLERBECK: I hope it is there though, mind.

EXT. COUNTRY LANE. DAY
BIRKIN *trudging through the rain. The handle of his Fish-Bass
gives way. He consults his map. He has reached the end of the lane,
stops, stares.*

EXT. CHURCH. DAY
The church is isolated among fields. Cut to BIRKIN *staring at it. He
smiles slightly as if in appreciation. Begins to walk towards it.
Then, as if realizing something, he breaks into a run. He reaches the
graveyard gate, fumbles loose the loop on it and begins to run around
the building. As he does so, a man,* KEACH, *approaches up
laneway, carrying an umbrella, stares incredulously towards*
BIRKIN. BIRKIN *stares up at gutters and pipes around the church,
anxiously. He finally smiles with relief, turns, goes towards the
portico.*

INT. CHURCH. DAY
BIRKIN *enters church, stands breathing heavily, stares around him,
then moves towards scaffolding.*

EXT. CHURCH. DAY
KEACH *enters portico, folds his umbrella and goes into the church.*

INT. CHURCH. DAY
KEACH: What were you doing?
BIRKIN: Um . . . um?
KEACH: Just now. Outside.
BIRKIN: Oh. Ch–ch–ch–checking the rain g–g–g–gutters. The
    down pipes.
KEACH: Why?
BIRKIN: Because if they were no g–g–good, there'll be no p–p–
    p–point my bothering to come in. It would have been d–d–
    d–destroyed, you see.
KEACH: Oh. Well, if you had waited to ask me I could have told
    you that they're all functioning perfectly. You could have
    saved yourself a run in the rain.
    (KEACH *closes door behind him. It squeals.*)
    (*Out of shot*) I'm Keach by the way. (*Little pause.*) Of
    course.

73

BIRKIN: Mmmmm?

(BIRKIN *turns and sees* KEACH.)

KEACH: The Reverend J. G. Keach. I'm the one who wrote to you. If you're Mr Birkin, that is. I take it you are.

BIRKIN: Oh, yes.

(*They shake hands.*)

KEACH: At what time . . . ah . . . did you leave London?

BIRKIN: At Te–te–te– Eleven o'clock.

(KEACH *looks at Birkin's belongings, which he has put on the floor.*)

KEACH: I see that in your – your anxiety to look at the gutters you didn't take time to drop your things off. Where have you decided to stay?

BIRKIN: Well, I th–th–thought – here.

KEACH: Here! (*Looking around*) Where here?

BIRKIN: Wh–what about the belfry?

KEACH: The belfry?

(BIRKIN *nods. His cheek begins to twitch. Obviously trying not to look at* BIRKIN's *twitch.*) Well . . . (*Gives a little laugh.*) I can't say that appeals to me. Having someone live in the belfry. Can't you take lodgings? Or a room at the Shepherd's Arms?

BIRKIN: I'm short of m–m–m– (*Stops.*) A bit short, you see.

KEACH: Oh. Well, I suppose in that case – but I should warn you that Mossop rings the bell for Sunday Service and the rope passes through a hole in the belfry floor.

BIRKIN: Th–th–th–th–th–

(BIRKIN *gets caught in hideous and prolonged stammer.* KEACH's *face during this.* BIRKIN *stops himself. Pause. Silence between them.*)

I don't mind.

KEACH: Very well, then. Now, what period do you suppose it to be?

BIRKIN: P–p–period?

KEACH: The mural. The wall-painting.

BIRKIN: Oh. (*Looking towards the scaffolding, taking it in*) I would g–g–guess about 1430 because of the Black Death. Survivors avoided hell fire by d–d–donating wall-paintings to churches. But I won't be able to say for sure until I've

unc–c–covered some of it. The c–c–clothes will give an
indication, of course. Whether they're wearing snoods,
which were later, or k–k–k–k– (*Stops. Little pause.*) Kirtles.

KEACH: Kirtles. So anyway about 1430. We shan't entertain any
extras.

BIRKIN: There won't be any.

KEACH: There *mustn't* be any. You agreed to twenty-five
guineas. Twelve pounds ten shillings to be paid halfway
and thirteen pounds fifteen shillings when finished and
approved by the executors.

BIRKIN: B–b–but not you?

KEACH: Mmmm?

BIRKIN: Not ap–ap–ap– I don't need your approval then?

KEACH: Miss Hebron omitted my name from the form of
bequest. An oversight, of course. However, to all intents
and purposes, I represent the executors. So you answer to
them through me. I shan't mind if you touch it up. Any
faint areas or even bits which may have disappeared. You
can fill them in. So long as it's appropriate and tones in
with the rest.

(BIRKIN'*s face is controlled, except for slight twitch.*)

BIRKIN: (*Incredulously*) T–t–touch up?

KEACH: Yes.

BIRKIN: So that it t–t–tones in?

(BIRKIN *stares at* KEACH, *laughs. Checks his laugh.*)
Of course, it isn't absolutely sure there's anything there.

KEACH: Of course there's something there. I may have a certain
reservation – which I'm not prepared to discuss – about
Miss Hebron but she was no fool. She went up a ladder
and scraped a patch until she found something.

(BIRKIN'*s face begins to twitch.*)

BIRKIN: (*Even more incredulous*) Sc–sc–sc–scraped? How b–b–
big a patch?

KEACH: One head, I believe. Certainly no more than two.

(BIRKIN *looks towards the wall.*)
Then she whitewashed it over again. You might as well
know here and now that your employment doesn't have my
support. But as the solicitors refuse to pay out her one-
thousand-pound bequest to our fabric fund until you've

done your job, I have no choice. (*Little pause.*) When the painting's uncovered it will be in full view of the congregation. It will distract from worship.

BIRKIN: After a t–t–t–t–time they won't notice it.

(KEACH *thinks, shakes his head.*)

KEACH: It will distract.

(KEACH *stares at* BIRKIN. BIRKIN *stares back.*)

Well, Mr Birkin, I'll leave you to settle into your quarters. Good night.

(KEACH *goes to the door, opens it. It squeals. He closes it. It squeals.* BIRKIN *smiles to himself. He turns and looks at the scaffolding and above it the blank white wall. He goes to his belongings, picks them up and we follow him up the stairs of the belfry.*)

INT. BELFRY. DUSK

BIRKIN *puts his belongings down, goes to the window. He takes out of his pocket a cigarette packet, extracts a half-cigarette, lights it. We see from his point of view rain still falling. Late evening, countryside dim and grey. Pick out, from his point of view a bell tent, in fact Moon's tent, in the field opposite. Beyond the field, the village. A man –* MOON *– emerges from the tent, stares up at the sky briefly, goes back into tent. Stay on tent, field, etc., then mix into shot of same point of view, night. Lights from the village very sparse. The light goes out in the bell tent.* BIRKIN *pulls his coat across the window, which is glassless. His oil lamp is on. He lies on his bed, smoking, calm.*

BIRKIN: (*Quietly*) Oxgodby.

(BIRKIN *smiles. Fade into* BIRKIN *asleep, restless, turning. He jerks up, lets out a howl. We stay on his face, fear-stricken.*)

INT. BELFRY. MORNING

BIRKIN *tottering to the window in the semi-darkness. He pulls his coat away from the window. Sunlight explodes into the room.* BIRKIN *recoils. Adjusting to the light, he looks out.*

EXT. MEADOW. MORNING
A marvellous morning, landscape, field, bell tent, etc. MOON
smoking a pipe, staring happily up at the sky. BIRKIN *turns away.*

EXT. TOMBSTONE. MORNING
Mug and water on tombstone. BIRKIN *finishing shaving in the sun.*
His hand is trembling slightly.

EXT. VILLAGE STREET. DAY
BIRKIN *walks up the street, passes* DOUTHWAITE *working in his*
blacksmith's forge. He nods to BIRKIN, *who nods back. A* MAN *on*
crutches walks past him. BIRKIN *enters small Post Office, which is*
also the local store. In the corner a young man, blind, (obviously
from the war) is sitting.
Several people talking in there fall silent, at the stranger's arrival.
BIRKIN *picks up the* Daily Mail, *takes money from his pocket, looks*
anxiously at how little he has, decides to buy cigarettes.

BIRKIN: (*To the woman behind the counter*) A pa–pa–pa–packet
   of ci–ci–ci–
   (BIRKIN *can't finish the word. He stops, defeated, amid*
   glances. Pays for the newspaper.)
   Th–th–th–thank you.
   (BIRKIN *leaves.*)

INT. CHURCH. MORNING
BIRKIN *climbing scaffolding, carrying workcase, putting the case*
down. BIRKIN *looks at the wall, runs his hands like a blind man*
across it. He stands for a moment, then opens the case. We see
bottles, containing alcoholic solution of hydrochloric acid, distilled
water, also brushes, dry colours, a lancet, various clothes. BIRKIN
extracts a cloth, takes out bottle of hydrochloric acid. Pours liquid on
to cloth, and makes to swab at wall. Looks at his hand. It is
shaking slightly. Sound of the door squealing open, footsteps.
BIRKIN *turns, sees* MOON *below, pulling squashed hat off head.*

MOON: Good morning, good morning, I'm Charles Moon. I'm
   the chap in the bell tent in the field opposite. I'd meant to
   let you settle in but I felt I *had* to come and have a look at

you. Well, partly that, but really because I get so stiff in the night my legs force me up, so I stump across most mornings to see if Laetitia's managed to climb out during the night.

(MOON *looks towards her cataflaque. We see Cojugam Optima Amantissima et delectissima.*)

Oh, most loving and delightful wife. I can never make out if that is grief or relief. (*Laughs.*) Do you mind if I come up for a moment?

(BIRKIN *hesitates.*)

I won't if you think I'm invading.

BIRKIN: C—come up.

(MOON *climbs the scaffold, stands beside* BIRKIN.)

MOON: You think there's something there?

BIRKIN: I hope so.

MOON: Good. We live by hope. And what do you think you'll find?

BIRKIN: A Judgement, I expect.

MOON: Ah, yes, a Judgement, that's what it would be, wouldn't it? Judgements always got the plum spots. So the whole parish could see the God-awful things that happened to them if they didn't fork out their tithes or marry the girls they'd got with child. St Michael weighing souls, Christ in Majesty refereeing and, down below, the Fire that flameth evermore, eh? Look, why don't you come over and have a cup of tea before you start?

(BIRKIN *looks towards the cloth, the wall-painting. Checks his hand.* MOON *sees this.*)

(*Grinning*) Come on. You've got the whole summer. Spin out the anticipation another half an hour, why don't you?

(BIRKIN *smiles, nods. Puts down cloth, etc.*)

EXT. MEADOW. DAY

MOON *and* BIRKIN *walking across the meadow, turning towards the tent.*

MOON: . . . so officially I'm looking for the grave of Miss Hebron's forebear, one Piers Hebron, born 1373. He was excommunicated. Buried somewhere outside the graveyard.

Miss Hebron set aside fifty pounds in her will for a chap like me to find out where, and get him back into consecrated ground. All I have to do is spend three or four weeks digging for his bones, and if I don't find them –
(MOON *gestures*.)

BIRKIN: You'll have wasted your t–t–t–time.
(MOON *stops, looks at* BIRKIN.)

MOON: Wasted my time? Good God, man, can't you see? (*Sweeps an arm around the meadow*.) I'm not here for Piers's bones, I'm here for a major discovery. My dear chap, we're standing on top of a basilica. A Saxon chapel. Probably goes back to 600. I spotted it the moment I got here. I've already come across a couple of cremation jars. There must be hundreds of them. You'll keep quiet about it, though, won't you? I don't want anyone to tumble to what I'm up to until I've got all I want and written it up.

BIRKIN: So you're be–be–being paid for one job and doing another?

MOON: That's right. Why not, if it's money well spent? And I'll leave a bit of time to prod around for the bones before I leave. I'll find them, don't you worry.
(*They have reached the tent*. MOON *pulls open the flap. It is pitched over a deep pit.* BIRKIN *almost falls into it.* MOON *catches him*.)
You were over there too. (*Pause*.) I can tell. That's where you developed your twitch and tremor and stammer, eh? Well, I developed a great affection for holes.
(MOON *jumps down. As* BIRKIN *follows he sees an open trunk with Moon's clothes and personal effects jumbled inside. Among them* BIRKIN *spots a Military Cross*.)
They make me feel safe, and they keep me insulated.
(*Pulls away a piece of sacking to expose an object*.) Here you are. My latest cremation jar. Come and have a look.
(BIRKIN *gets down as the tent flap opens.* COLONEL *appears,* MOSSOP *slightly behind him at his shoulder*.)

COLONEL: Ah, Moon.
(MOON *turns quickly and stands to conceal the cremation jar, which is nevertheless glimpsed by* MOSSOP.)

MOON: Morning, Colonel. Morning, Mossop. (*Directed at*

BIRKIN) Colonel Hebron, Miss Hebron's brother. Mossop
looks after the church. This is Mr Birkin who's come to
uncover the painting.
COLONEL: Ah. Good. Well done. And what about you, Moon?
Making progress? Any sign of old Piers's bones yet?
(MOSSOP *looks around.*)
MOON: Not yet, Colonel.
COLONEL: Found anything out of the ordinary, gold or silver,
jugs and jars, etc.?
MOON: Wish I had.
COLONEL: Well, press on. Let me know.
(*Directed at* BIRKIN) Stay as long as you like. Care to
umpire for us on Saturdays? Mossop here says he can't do
it any more, on account of his legs. Well, would have liked
to loiter with you. Another morning perhaps. Must be on
my way. Things – (*His face goes blank.*) Things to do. So,
Mossop, there's your umpiring taken care of. (*Directed at*
BIRKIN) Very civil of you.
(*The* COLONEL *shambles off.* MOSSOP *fixes his eyes on the jar
suspiciously, just visible behind* MOON.)
MOSSOP: Th'a found some'at then.
MOON: Oh, just the usual artefact, I'm afraid, Mossop.
(MOON *is blocking* MOSSOP's *view.* MOSSOP *tries to peer
around him. Turns and plods off to church.* MOON *and*
BIRKIN *exchange smiles.*)

INT. CHURCH. DAY
We come in on BIRKIN's *hand. Slight tremor. Cut to* BIRKIN's *face
concentrating on steadying his hand. He is on the scaffolding at the
apex of the roof. He takes a deep breath. Begins work.* MOSSOP
sweeping around the floor, grimly. BIRKIN's *face concentrating. Cut
to wall: we see the head of Christ gradually emerging. Cut to*
BIRKIN's *face staring in concentration and take in his hand, now
controlled. Cut back to the head of Christ.* BIRKIN *stops work.*

INT. CHURCH. DAY
Several days later. MOON *and* BIRKIN. *Christ's face is now
distinct, sharp beard, drooping moustache, heavily lidded eyes visible
through the whitewash. Cut to* BIRKIN, *his face intense, leaning*

forward. Cut dramatically to face fully present and vivid. Cut to
MOON *staring at it.*

MOON: Yes, well he isn't out of the usual catalogue, is he? He's
a wintry hard-liner, your Christ. All justice and no mercy.
(*Cut to* BIRKIN *staring at the Christ.*)
No, I wouldn't fancy being in the dock, if he was the beak.
'And he shal com with wondes rede to deme the quikke
and the ded – '
(*Bell tolls over the image of Christ.*)

INT. BELFRY. DAY
Rope being pulled through the floor, bells very loud. BIRKIN *lying
in bed, eyes open, staring.*

INT. CHURCH. DAY
BIRKIN, *half dressed, looking down on congregation, from whom a
hymn thinly rises.*

KEACH: (*Voice over, from below, just audible*) Let us pray.
(*The congregation kneels and* BIRKIN'S *eye travels along past*
KEACH *and up to take in the wall, the image of Christ.*)
BIRKIN: (*Aloud as* KEACH's *voice drones on*) Look behind you,
Keach. That's what you're praying to but he doesn't want
your prayers, he wants some answers. Did you f–f–fede the
hongry? Did you give d–d–drynke to the thirsty? Did you
c–c–clothe the naked and nedye, h–h–herbowre the
houseless, comfort the s–s–seke, visit the prisoners? And
what about me, eh? Did any of you offer me bed and
board?
(*The congregation rises. Organ sound over. The hymn begins.*)
Yes, you smug Yorkshire lot. I'll have a word with Him
about the way you've treated me. He'll g–g–g–et you yet.
(*Grins.*) And so will I.
(BIRKIN *looks down, notices* MRS KEACH *in her pew, with
hat, half profile.* BIRKIN *doesn't see her full face. She doesn't
see him. Hymn weedily continues.*)

INT. CHURCH. DAY
BIRKIN *on scaffold, working. Sound over of door squealing,*
shutting, footsteps.

KATHY: (*Out of shot*) Hello there, Mr Birkin.
(BIRKIN *turns, and sees from his point of view* KATHY *and*
EDGAR.)
BIRKIN: Hello.
(BIRKIN *returns to his work, paying no attention to the two*
below. KATHY *is carrying packages of food.* EDGAR, *with*
great difficulty, a gramophone and records. EDGAR *puts them*
down. KATHY *puts on a record: 'Angels ever bright and fair /*
Take, O take me to your care'. BIRKIN *turns and looks down*
in surprise.)
KATHY: I'm Kathy Ellerbeck. And this is my brother, Edgar.
Our dad's the stationmaster. We've brought you a rabbit
pie. Our mam says you'll need the nourishment.
BIRKIN: Thank you.
EDGAR: Our dad says you must be miserable working all day on
your own up there, so he said we could play you some
records. (*Directed at* KATHY) Didn't he?
(*Cut to* BIRKIN *working as record, at various stages, comes*
scratching to a halt.)
KATHY: Can we come up now?
BIRKIN: Sorry. No one's allowed up. That's an ab–ab–absolute
rule.
KATHY: What about Mr Moon? Mr Mossop says you let him
up.
BIRKIN: Ah, well. We have a re–re–reciprocal agreement. He
looks at my work and I look at his.
KATHY: Can we stay down here then?
BIRKIN: As long as you don't mind my t–t–turning my back on
you. But why do you want to?
KATHY: My dad said you were an opportunity that mightn't
come again in a little spot like this – watching an artist at
work.
BIRKIN: Ah, but I'm not an artist. I'm the labourer who cleans
up after artists.

EDGAR: We have a picture painted on our chapel wall. Behind the pulpit.

KATHY: Three big arum lilies. It's very beautiful.

BIRKIN: Why?

KATHY: Why what?

BIRKIN: Why is it lilies? Why just lilies? Why not lilies and roses or just roses? Or roses and d–d–daisies?

KATHY: Because underneath it says, 'Consider the lilies' in old-fashioned lettering. It's a text. 'Consider the lilies how they grow. They toil not – ' You know.

BIRKIN: I do. It's in support of malingering. I wouldn't have thought you Ch–ch–chapelers would agree with that.

KATHY: (*After a little pause*) Mam wanted one of roses, with 'By cool Siloam's shady rill' under it. But in the end Dad and Mr Douthwaite decided on the lilies. Because of the congregation.

BIRKIN: But why? Why couldn't they look at roses or d–d–daisies?

KATHY: (*Savagely*) Oh, I don't know!

(KATHY *seizes the record, turns it over and winds up the gramophone. She listens for a moment, watching* BIRKIN. *Cut to* BIRKIN, *working, over 'O for the Wings of a Dove'*.)

EXT. CHURCH GRAVEYARD. NOON
Pies, scones, bread, etc. Take in MOON *and* BIRKIN *eating contentedly in the graveyard.*

MOON: From the stationmaster's wife, eh?

BIRKIN: That's right, her children brought it.

(MOON *takes a large bite out of the pie, savouring it.*)

MOON: And what has the Rev J. G. Keach brought you?

BIRKIN: Nothing.

MOON: No money yet?

(BIRKIN *shakes his head.* MOON *takes out his pipe and looks at* BIRKIN.)

(*Shyly*) Oh, by the way, you said the other day something about longing for a Woodbine. Well – (*Takes out of his pocket a packet of Woodbines.*) Look what I dug up this morning.

(MOON *hands the packet to* BIRKIN.)

BIRKIN: (*Taking it*) Thanks.

(*They smoke contentedly as we watch from the point of view of the belfry window.* MOON *gets up and walks towards the field. Cut back to* BIRKIN *still sitting, smoking. We see from his point of view as if hazily, close to sleep,* MOON's *retreating figure.* BIRKIN *gets up slowly, goes to box tomb, lies down on it, puts his handkerchief over his eyes. Long shot of the graveyard with* BIRKIN *asleep, on tomb.*)

EXT. GRAVEYARD. EARLY AFTERNOON

ALICE KEACH's *face, hazy, slightly out of focus.* BIRKIN, *blinking, staring at her, the handkerchief slipped down.* MRS KEACH *wearing a wide-brimmed straw hat that casts a shadow across her face.*

MRS KEACH: Oh, I'm sorry, did I wake you?

BIRKIN: That depends on wh–wh–whether I'm awake. (*Sits up.*) Have you been here long?

MRS KEACH: Maybe ten minutes. I'm not sure. I'm Alice Keach. I just wanted to find out if you were all right in the bell loft, or if there's anything you needed. It seems so – so inhospitable, we in our beds and you up there on the floorboards. We've got a travelling rug.

BIRKIN: No, I'm all right, thank you. At the end of the day I'm so tired I sleep like the d–d–dead. And d–d–during the day too, sometimes.

(BIRKIN *laughs, gesturing to the box tomb.*)

MRS KEACH: Oh. Well then –

(*Vaguely, she looks around, sees* MOON, *in the meadow, doing an odd dance. She watches puzzled.*)

BIRKIN: He's working off his cramp.

MRS KEACH: Oh.

(MRS KEACH *steps forward.* BIRKIN *sees her face properly for the first time.*)

The painting. When will we be able to see all of it?

BIRKIN: Well, I don't know really. It's a bit like a jigsaw. A face, a shoe, here a bit, there a bit.

MRS KEACH: Oh.

BIRKIN: It comes together very slowly. If it comes together at all. But of course after f–f–f–f–
(MRS KEACH's *face. Cut back to* BIRKIN. *Slight pause.*)
(*Desperately*) F–f–five hundred years I can't be sure what I'll f–f–f–f–

MRS KEACH: But that's the exciting part, isn't it? Not knowing what's around the corner. Like opening a parcel at Christmas. (*Laughs.*) So you must let me see it, Mr Birkin, because Christmas is for everybody. Anyway, I'll haunt you a little until you do.
(MRS KEACH *begins to move away.*)

BIRKIN: Are you by any chance related to the Reverend J. G. K–Keach, the vicar?

MRS KEACH: I'm his wife.

BIRKIN: Oh.
(BIRKIN *smiles and nods.* MRS KEACH *turns, walks across the meadow, passes* MOON, *who lifts his hat.* MRS KEACH *nods, smiles.* BIRKIN *watches.* MOON *comes up to him.*)

MOON: A stunner, isn't she?

BIRKIN: Is she?

MOON: Of course she is. And you know it. Come on, admit you do.
(*Cut to* MRS KEACH *from their point of view walking across meadow.*)

BIRKIN: Oh, I admit it. But per–per–perhaps she wouldn't. Perhaps she doesn't even know it.

MOON: Rubbish! Every woman knows if she's beautiful. And think of Keach catching her. Of all people. You're married too, aren't you?

BIRKIN: Sort of. (*Pause.*) She went off with another chap. Not for the first time. Can't really blame her, I suppose. Her name's Vinny.

MOON: Thought it might be something like that. As for me, never met the right woman. Luckily for her.
(MOON *laughs. Turns to* BIRKIN, *but there's something uneasy in his eyes.* MRS KEACH *walks away in the distance.* BIRKIN *looks away from* MOON, *looks after* MRS KEACH.)

INT. CHURCH. DAY
Some days later. Cut to BIRKIN *working on painting, uncovering particularly ugly devil-like face as, over, 'O for the Wings of a Dove' coming to an end. The record whirrs to a stop.*

KATHY: (*Out of shot*) That's all for today, Mr Birkin.
BIRKIN: (*Abstractedly*) Oh, right.
KATHY: (*Out of shot*) Oh, Mam and Dad say you've got to come to lunch on Sunday.
BIRKIN: What?
    (BIRKIN *turns, looks down. We see* KATHY *and* EDGAR *from his point of view.*)
EDGAR: You're coming to lunch on Sunday.
BIRKIN: Oh, well, thank you.
KATHY: Oh, Mr Douthwaite will be coming too, the blacksmith. He comes most Sundays.
BIRKIN: Right. Well, thank you.
    (KATHY *nods. She and* EDGAR *turn to leave.*)
    Oh, but what time?
KATHY: Eleven o'clock, of course.
BIRKIN: Eleven o'clock?
KATHY: Yes, at the chapel. It starts at eleven.
    (*Cut to* BIRKIN'*s face.*)

EXT./INT. CHAPEL. DAY
We come in on ELLERBECK, *in the pulpit, staring ferociously out.*

ELLERBECK: (*Bellowing*) Brethren and fellow sinners!
    (*He slams his fist down on the pulpit; the water decanter leaps.*)
    Yea, sinners, I say 'sinners', for are we all not hereunto sinners?
    (*Cut to* MRS ELLERBECK *sitting, head lowered,* KATHY *and* EDGAR *staring up at* ELLERBECK.)
    Is there one among you here who can say he isn't a sinner? Is there? If so, I challenge him to come forward and speak.
    (*He gazes around. Finally settles his gaze on* BIRKIN. *Cut to* BIRKIN'*s face.*)

INT. ELLERBECK KITCHEN. DAY
Later. We come in on the kitchen table. ELLERBECK, MRS
ELLERBECK, DOUTHWAITE, KATHY, EDGAR *and* BIRKIN
standing, heads lowered around it. There is a pause. DOUTHWAITE
is thinking. He is in fact in the middle of Grace.

DOUTHWAITE: So what it comes to, Lord, is that we accept
with thanks all the provisions you provided for Mr and Mrs
Ellerbeck, Kathy, Edgar, Mr Birkin and myself, and would
like you to know that as we settle down to our meal we are
holding you with love in our hearts because we know,
Lord, that if it weren't for you, we wouldn't have a meal
and furthermore we wouldn't be here in the first place.
(*Thinks again.*) So thank you, Lord.

INT. ELLERBECK KITCHEN. DAY
Later. Close on ELLERBECK's *hands sharpening a knife, a virtuoso
performance, steel crashing together, up to* ELLERBECK's *face, back
to knife and steel, as he comes to a flourishing conclusion.*

ELLERBECK: My father was a butcher, Mr Birkin.
(*Cut to* BIRKIN *sitting with* MRS ELLERBECK, KATHY *and*
EDGAR *as they sit around a huge Sunday joint.*)

INT. ELLERBECK FRONT ROOM. DAY
After lunch. ELLERBECK *asleep in chair.* DOUTHWAITE *asleep in
chair.* MRS ELLERBECK *sewing,* BIRKIN *sitting drowsy.* KATHY *at
the table, reading.* EDGAR *drawing. Silence, except for sleeping
noises from* ELLERBECK. BIRKIN *looks at* ELLERBECK, *then* MRS
ELLERBECK, *who smiles at him, then he looks vaguely ahead.*
ELLERBECK *wakes up with a start.*

ELLERBECK: Well, it's Barton Terry for me this afternoon,
Mother.
MRS ELLERBECK: Does it have to be you? You're tired out. At
your age you should be having a lie-down, not doing that
long walk in the sun.
KATHY: And the last time you went you came back all faint,
didn't he, Mam?

DOUTHWAITE: I'd do it for you, William, except that I promised I'd go and help out at Grimsley Sunday School.

ELLERBECK: No, that's all right, George, I'll manage.

KATHY: Mr Birkin here will go for you, won't you, Mr Birkin?

BIRKIN: (*Blinking*) What? Go where?

KATHY: We'll show you.

MRS ELLERBECK: (*Directed at* MR ELLERBECK.) Well, what do you say?

ELLERBECK: Well, there's no denying that Mr Birkin's legs are younger than mine.

MRS ELLERBECK: You wouldn't mind going, would you, Mr Birkin?

BIRKIN: But to do what?

ELLERBECK: Oh, just a bit of preaching.

BIRKIN: But I've never p–p–preached in my life.

ELLERBECK: (*Comfortably*) Well, you heard me this morning. Just do that.

KATHY: (*Grinning*) Yes, just do what Dad does.

EDGAR: Yes.

INT. BARTON TERRY CHAPEL. AFTERNOON
We come in on BIRKIN *in the most enormous pulpit and take in from his point of view* LUCY SYKES *at the organ and a congregation consisting of several old men, an old lady, a few farm lads and* KATHY *and* EDGAR. *Cut back to* BIRKIN.

BIRKIN: Brethren and – and (*feebly*) fellow sinners um – let us – um – p–p–p–pray.
(*He lowers his head, mutters vaguely, lifts his head, pats the front of pulpit, looks around.*)
My sermon today derives – derives – (*Little pause.*) Oh, look here, I only came in place of Mr Ellerbeck because he's – he's indisposed. I can't preach. (*Little pause. Swallows.*) All I can talk to you about is what I'm up to in Oxgodby. In the church there. And – and if you want to leave or nod off that's all right by me.
(*The congregation stares up at* BIRKIN *with curiosity.*)
You see, I'm cleaning the wall there. The one above the nave. Because behind the dirt and the layers of paint is a p–

p–picture. So there I am, you see, up there on my s–
scaffolding, cleaning away until I get back to the painting
itself. It's like – like prising open a window in a filthy wall.
Every day or so I open it a square foot or so wider. It's
really all patience, you see, my sort of work. But I don't
get any second chances. That's what makes it so exciting.
One dab too few and some poor chap won't get back from
five centuries ago. One dab too many and I'll have wiped
him out for ever. Oh, that makes me sound rather like
God, doesn't it?
(*The congregation stares up at him, expressionlessly. Cut back
to* BIRKIN.)
But really I'm just a servant like every one of us. Except
that I'm the servant of the painter. I hope I'm good enough
to serve him because this painter deserves the best of
servants. (*Little pause.*) Now I'll tell you about my tools.
What I basically use is a lancet – that's for lifting off the
limewash. Then I have alcoholic solution of hydrochloric
acid –

EXT. OUTSIDE CHAPEL. AFTERNOON
*We come in on the elderly from the congregation, the old man in
front. Pause on his face. Cut to* BIRKIN'*s face, apprehensive, and
cut back to the old man's face. The old man nods acknowledgement,
turns away, the others following him.* BIRKIN *stares after them,
then turns to* KATHY *and* EDGAR *as* LUCY SYKES, *in shot, locks
the chapel door.*

KATHY: (*To* EDGAR) They liked it, didn't they?
EDGAR: But our Dad's louder.
　　　(LUCY SYKES *approaches. Little pause.*)
LUCY: You could come and have your tea.
BIRKIN: Well, I – I came with these two.
LUCY: They can come too.

INT. SYKES PARLOUR. AFTERNOON
MR SYKES, MRS SYKES, LUCY SYKES, KATHY *and* EDGAR *and*
BIRKIN *in the farmhouse parlour. Window open, butterflies visible,*

drowsy heat without. Within, they are eating tea. A piano, a photograph on top of it.

SYKES: (*After a pause*) You're from London then, Mr Birkin?
BIRKIN: Yes. (*Little pause.*) London. That's right.
MRS SYKES: We've never met a Londoner before.
SYKES: You're our first, Mr Birkin.
BIRKIN: Oh.
    (*Pause.* LUCY *glances at him shyly, smiles.* BIRKIN *smiles tentatively back. This is observed by* KATHY.)
SYKES: (*Out of shot*) You were over there, were you, Mr Birkin? In France?
    (BIRKIN *nods.*)
MRS SYKES: So was our Perce.
    (MRS SYKES *nods towards the photograph of a young man on the piano.* BIRKIN *looks at the photograph. The young man is stocky, smiling.*)
    (*Out of shot*) He had it taken on his last leave. His nineteenth birthday.
SYKES: (*Out of shot*) He was a right good lad, Perce. A real worker. Would give anybody a hand. They all liked him.
    (BIRKIN'*s face staring at the photograph.* SYKES, MRS SYKES, *staring at him.* LUCY'*s face, very quickly turning slightly away.*)
    (*Attempting joviality*) Well, would you like to see the farm, Mr Birkin?
MRS SYKES: Yes. Lucy, why don't you show Mr Birkin around the farm?
LUCY: (*To* KATHY *and* EDGAR) Would you like to see around?
KATHY: We can't. We've got to visit Emily Clough. (*To* BIRKIN) We promised her and we told our Sunday School teacher we'd take her her star card.
BIRKIN: Emily Clough?
KATHY: We said we'd bring you too. She's expecting you. (*To* EDGAR) Isn't she?
EDGAR: Yes.
    (*There is an uncertain pause.* BIRKIN *clearly at sea.* KATHY *obviously determined.*)

MRS SYKES: Oh well, perhaps another Sunday.
(LUCY *smiles at* BIRKIN.)

EXT. CLOUGH COTTAGE. AFTERNOON
The cottage door open.

INT. CLOUGH COTTAGE: HALLWAY. AFTERNOON
KATHY *in the hall,* BIRKIN *and* EDGAR *behind her.*

KATHY: Mrs Clough, Mrs Clough, we've come to bring Emily
some flowers.
(MRS CLOUGH *appears at the door of the kitchen at the end of
the hallway.*)
MRS CLOUGH: Go on up. On your way out you can have a jam
tart.
(*She looks at* BIRKIN *as he pauses at bottom of stairs. She is
grief-stricken and turns away quickly.* BIRKIN *understands.*)

INT. EMILY CLOUGH'S BEDROOM. DAY
*Cut to an apple tree, seen through the window, a sense of oppressive
heat. Then drift to Edgar's flowers, in a jar beside a bed, to which
we drift next, and* EMILY'S *face, luminously pale.*

KATHY: (*Out of shot*) I've brought your star card, Emily. Mr
Douthwaite stamped it S for sick. S's count the same as
stars.
(*Cut to* EMILY.)
You only need six more stars for a prize.
EDGAR: Or S's for sick.
EMILY: I've been thinking about my prize. I like *The Forgotten
Garden.* Can Mr Douthwaite get me one by the same
author? What are you having?
KATHY: *The Coral Island.* And Edgar's having *Children of the
New Forest.*
BIRKIN: Isn't that a bit beyond him?
KATHY: He'll grow to like it later. I've heard it's a good story
with two girls in it. Mr Birkin's the man living in the
church, Emily.
EMILY: I've heard about you. I hope you'll still be there when

I'm up, Mr Birkin. I like your straw hat, Kathy. Can I try
it on?
(KATHY *takes off the straw hat, hands it to* EMILY. EMILY
*puts the hat on, turns to the mirror. She is suddenly racked by a
tubercular cough. She presses a handkerchief to her mouth on
which spots of blood appear. She recovers and smiles weakly.*)
I think it suits me. I like hats. Wearing a hat's part of the
fun at Sunday School.

EDGAR: When you come next you can wear it, can't she, Kathy?
(EMILY *looks at* BIRKIN. *Their eyes meet.*)

EXT. CLOUGH COTTAGE. AFTERNOON
BIRKIN *and* KATHY *walking down the road,* EDGAR *to one side,
picking flowers.*

KATHY: (*Out of shot*) She knows she's dying, doesn't she?
(*Fade on them receding down the road.*)

INT. ELLERBECK FRONT PARLOUR. LATER
We come in on BIRKIN *sitting, remote. He has his hand covering his
cheek. Very slight tremble in the hand.* ELLERBECK, MRS
ELLERBECK, KATHY *and* EDGAR *with cups of tea.*

MRS ELLERBECK: Are you all right, Mr Birkin? You haven't
touched your tea.
KATHY: (*Smiling slightly unpleasantly*) He had his tea at Lucy
Sykes'. She asked us in.
MRS ELLERBECK: She's a fine strong girl, Lucy Sykes.
ELLERBECK: That's right. Good Christian upbringing too.
MRS ELLERBECK: Time we asked her along to the Sunday
School outing, eh, Father?
ELLERBECK: Aye. I meant to last year –
(BIRKIN, *clearly not taking this in, suddenly gets up,
interrupting, his face twitching slightly.*)
BIRKIN: P–p–please excuse me. I have a g–g–g–g– must get
back.
(*He puts his hand to his face.*)
KATHY: (*As* BIRKIN *leaves; out of shot, confidentially*) It's that
Lucy Sykes. He's been funny ever since he saw her.

EXT. VILLAGE. LATER
Cut to BIRKIN *walking through the village. As he does so, he passes the blind young man sitting on the doorstep.* BIRKIN, *glancing at him, continues walking, his face set.*

EXT. MOON'S FIELD. EVENING
BIRKIN *walking past Moon's tent towards the church. From the church suddenly sound of hymn thinly: 'O God our Help in Ages Past'. Evensong.* BIRKIN *stops. Stares at the church.*

BIRKIN: (*Screaming suddenly*) God? What God? There is no God.
(*Behind him,* MOON *comes out of his tent.* BIRKIN, *as if suddenly aware, turns. He and* MOON *look at each other.*)

INT. CHURCH. DAY
BIRKIN *at work.* MRS KEACH *arrives in the church.*

BIRKIN: I don't really want 'Angels Bright and Fair' this morning, if you don't mind.
MRS KEACH: Well, will you accept my travelling rug?
BIRKIN: I'm sorry. I thought you were someone else.
MRS KEACH: Yes, I know. Kathy Ellerbeck and her gramophone.
(MRS KEACH *puts the rug down on Laetitia's tomb.*)
Now you'll have to let me come up. That's our agreement. (*Pause.*) May I? (*Starts to climb.*) Mr Moon said he was sure you wouldn't let me, that you wanted to keep it all to yourself.
(MRS KEACH, *her face upturned, seen from* BIRKIN's *point of view. He holds out his hand tentatively. She takes it, steps off the ladder. Just for a second their eyes meet. She turns to the painting. We see her expression change. Cut to painting.*
BIRKIN *watches her. She is clearly shocked by the Bosch-like images of hell and suffering.*)
Why, it's a sort of – a sort of hell. Horrible.
BIRKIN: Well, probably not so horrible if you believed in it.
MRS KEACH: And do you believe in it, Mr Birkin?

BIRKIN: When I look at it – when I'm working on it I believe in his belief. Impossible not to really.

MRS KEACH: But otherwise you don't believe there is a hell?

BIRKIN: Well, I suppose hell means different things to different people.

MRS KEACH: What does it mean to you?

BIRKIN: (*Slight smile.*) Hell on earth, I think.

MRS KEACH: (*Thinks; realizes.*) Yes, of course. Although I don't understand really, how could I?

BIRKIN: Why should you?

MRS KEACH: I suppose one should try.

BIRKIN: (*Suddenly blurting out*) No, you shouldn't. I'd rather you didn't.

> (*There is a pause.* MRS KEACH *makes to say something, says instead*:)

MRS KEACH: Were you always in the cleaning business, Mr Birkin?

> (BIRKIN *nods.*)

> How did you come by it?

BIRKIN: It's in the f–family. My father travelled in s–s–soap.

> (*He looks at her seriously. She looks back, then begins to laugh.* BIRKIN *smiles. She goes to the ladder. Begins to go down it.* BIRKIN *makes to say something, obviously to offer to accompany her, checks himself.*)

MRS KEACH: Thank you.

> (BIRKIN *is puzzled.*)

> For letting me see.

> (*We see* MRS KEACH *walking across the church from* BIRKIN'S *point of view. The door squealing as she goes out.*)

EXT. VILLAGE PUB. DAY

Later. Opposite the pub is the chapel. BIRKIN *and* MOON *are sitting on the bench outside the Shepherd's Arms. As they talk,* PEOPLE *are entering the chapel. Among them the* ELLERBECKS, *who don't see* BIRKIN *and* MOON.

MOON: (*With an expression of strain, in the pause of a painful speech*) I half wanted it to happen. There were times when I'd had enough. Well, you know that. I mean – when I was sure my nerve would give way and I'd lie down before I was hit. Or worse. Wouldn't be able to drive myself over the top, ever again. So many had gone. Chaps I cared for. Sometimes it seemed they were the lucky ones. (*Pause*.) The night's the bad time. Well, I expect you've heard me. I still wake up screaming. I can still see . . . still see . . . (*pause*) but I tell myself it'll be better as time passes and it sinks further back. But it's got nowhere to sink to, has it? We'll always be different, won't we, the whole lot of us? (*Little pause*.) All the millions of us that survived. If millions did. Different, I mean, from the generations before us who had no idea that anything like that could ever happen. I don't know if it's worse not having something to show for it. Like a lost limb or two or blindness. I mean, people like you and me, the intact ones. The worse part for me was the last part when I was kept away from the fighting. Went for months without seeing a single corpse. The faces I did see – (*stops*) – but I'm a little round the bend, you know. Always will be, I expect. (*Suddenly cheerful*) Still, there's no point in letting it get one down. One's got a life to lead anyway. (*Grins*.) 'And then he shal come with wondes rede to deme the quikke and the dede.'

BIRKIN: But you got the Military Cross, didn't you? I saw it in your tent.

MOON: Medals!

(*From the chapel the sudden crashing of an out-of-tune organ. Voices raised in a cheerful hymn.*)

Ah, there go the chapel lot. I wish they'd get themselves a new organ.

BIRKIN: (*Standing up*) I'll get us another –

(BIRKIN *begins to go into the pub. Puts his hand into his pocket, takes out a few coins, looks down at them, stops.*)

I'm sorry, I can't.

MOON: Keach still hasn't coughed up, eh? Then you'll just have to go and get it from him, won't you? Like a good soldier. Tell him you need it to drink a toast to that lost beauty, his wife. Tonight's on me. (*Gets up, then turns back.*) Did she get you to show her the painting? I saw her going into the church.

BIRKIN: Yes.

MOON: I told her you wouldn't, but I was sure you would.

(BIRKIN *stands, looks towards the chapel, from which comes the discordant hymn, voices even louder. He suddenly smiles.*)

BIRKIN: That's more like it.

EXT. VICARAGE. DAY

Seen from BIRKIN's *point of view at the edge of the clearing.* BIRKIN *walks across, knocks on the door. Knocks again. Seen in long shot, then we come in closer as he spots the bell. Pulls it out. Nothing. He pulls again, more savagely. From within the house a remote tinkle.* BIRKIN *pulls again. Tinkle continues.* BIRKIN *turns angrily, and cut to* MRS KEACH *standing on the drive by the porch, staring at him.*

BIRKIN: I've come to see your hus–hus–husband. But he isn't . . .

(*He gestures.*)

MRS KEACH: Oh, he wouldn't be able to hear you. He's playing. Right at the end of the house.

(*They go to the house up steps.*)

INT. VICARAGE: CORRIDOR. DAY

A long shot from inside the hallway of MRS KEACH *and* BIRKIN *as* MRS KEACH *opens the door.*

MRS KEACH: You haven't been here before, have you? We have it all to ourselves. (*Gives an odd little laugh.*) Of course it's much too big.

(*They begin to walk down the corridor. Faintly, the sound of a violin, playing a melancholy air. It gets stronger as they proceed towards it.*)

Most of the rooms are empty, you see. This one . . .

(*Touches the door as she passes.*) And this one – and this one – completely empty – this one . . .

(*They approach the room at end of the corridor, from which, evidently, the violin.* MRS KEACH *stops.*)

It can be quite oppressive. It gives me nightmares
sometimes. Well, the same nightmare really. Of the trees
outside closing in, and only the walls – these walls – to stop
them.

INT. VICARAGE: LIVING ROOM. DAY
At the end of the room, sparsely furnished, KEACH *is playing a
fiddle in front of a music stand. He continues playing, not seeing*
BIRKIN, *his eyes closed, an expression of concentrated rapture on his
face. He plays rather badly. Then he opens eyes, sees them. Stops.*

MRS KEACH: I found Mr Birkin on the doorstep. But you
  couldn't hear the bell.
KEACH: No, I suppose not. At least I didn't hear it.
MRS KEACH: We don't have many visitors, you see.
KEACH: Yes, one gets out of the habit of listening for them.
MRS KEACH: And I was just saying to Mr Birkin, such a big
  house, isn't it, for just the two of us?
KEACH: Yes, it is, really.
MRS KEACH: And all the rooms – we don't know what to put in
  them, do we?
  (MRS KEACH *gestures around the room.*)
KEACH: No, that's true.
  (BIRKIN *looks, nothing on the walls, the windows curtainless.
  His eyes take in the vacancy, then come to rest on a massive
  unidentifiable piece of furniture.*)
MRS KEACH: Except for that. At least it's big enough. But we
  don't know what it is or does. It seems to be part of
  something else. My husband's father bought it at an
  auction sale because no one else wanted it. To help fill the
  room, didn't he?
KEACH: That's right. He did.
  (BIRKIN *nods, hesitates.*)
BIRKIN: I just came to sort out the qu–qu–question of my mon–
  mon–mon–money.
  (KEACH *and* MRS KEACH *appear to be staring at him in
  horror. There is a pause, as the situation is held, then* BIRKIN
  turns. At the window, glaring in, a large cat, with a bloody

songbird in its mouth. The cat leaps off the window. BIRKIN
turns back. KEACH *looks at* BIRKIN *blankly. Then realizes.*)

KEACH: Oh, yes, the money. I suppose you brought the receipt,
Mr Birkin.

BIRKIN: The receipt?

KEACH: For the money.

BIRKIN: The mon–money?

KEACH: Yes, I sent Mossop with your first instalment this
morning. Didn't he give it to you?

BIRKIN: We must have passed each other. Thank you.
(KEACH *nods. Slight pause.*)

KEACH: Well, perhaps some refreshment.

BIRKIN: No, thank you, I'd better get back to work.

MRS KEACH: Did you come by the wood?

BIRKIN: No. The road.

MRS KEACH: I'll show you the way through the wood.

KEACH: When are you going to show my wife the painting?
She's very anxious to see it.

MRS KEACH: Oh, I've already seen it.

KEACH: Have you? I hadn't realized.

INT. VICARAGE: CORRIDOR. DAY

MRS KEACH *and* BIRKIN *walking down the corridor.* BIRKIN
opening the door as, over, sound of KEACH *on his violin.* BIRKIN
*glances back and we see from his point of view the door of room
open,* KEACH *playing his violin.* BIRKIN *closes the door on this
image.*

EXT. VICARAGE: GARDEN. DAY

BIRKIN *and* MRS KEACH *walk along the garden path towards the
woods.*

MRS KEACH: Do you like my roses, Mr Birkin? I spend a lot of
time on them. Though there isn't really anyone else to look
at them but me. This one's a Sarah van Fleet. It's a very
old variety.
(BIRKIN *looks, makes to pick one, hesitates.*)

BIRKIN: May I?

MRS KEACH: Mind. It has sharp thorns. (*Picks one.*) They keep

on blooming into autumn. So you'll know when summer's
ended because I always wear one of the last in my hat.
(MRS KEACH *hands the rose to* BIRKIN. BIRKIN *takes the
rose.*)

EXT. WOODS. DAY
A wood, almost unreal in its loveliness. BIRKIN *and* MRS KEACH
walking through it. Birds flying. BIRKIN *stops.*

BIRKIN: But this is beautiful. A kind of paradise.
MRS KEACH: (*Excited*) Look!
      (BIRKIN *looks. Just visible, a hare bounding.* BIRKIN *smiles.*)
BIRKIN: I think you're b–b–beau . . .
      (*Sudden sound of shot loud and close. The hare leaps and
      bounds off at great speed. Cut to* BIRKIN's *face. It is in spasm.
      His hand to his face, shaking. The* COLONEL *appears with a
      gun. Greets them cheerfully and walks on.* BIRKIN *brings
      himself under control. Slight pause.* BIRKIN *attempts a smile.*)
      Well, I suppose that's what comes of believing in paradise.
      (*He smiles.* MRS KEACH *smiles back. They part.*)

INT. BELFRY. NIGHT
Seemingly the same shot, though the light comes from an oil lamp.
BIRKIN *is sitting on the camp bed, but we come directly in on his
hand holding the rose. He puts it between the pages of a book.
Closes the book, and presses hard. Take in the cover: Scott-
Bradshaw:* A History of Church Architecture. *Continues to press
hard, puts book down beside the bed. Turns off the lamp. Holding
the book, crosses to the window, looks out.*

EXT. COUNTRYSIDE. NIGHT
Darkness. Lights twinkling in the village and in Moon's tent.
BIRKIN *stands at window, gazing out.*

EXT. GRAVEYARD/MOON'S TENT. NIGHT
Moonlight. Later. A sudden cry from Moon's tent.

INT. BELFRY. NIGHT
BIRKIN's *face, sympathetic.*

99

EXT. MOON'S TENT. NIGHT

Lights go on in the tent, shot of MOON *in silhouette, sitting bent, clutching his hands. Stay on Moon's tent, fading into shot of him standing in silhouette, putting out lamp. Cut to darkness. Fading into misty dawn. And cut to* BIRKIN's *face, still at window, looking out.*

INT./EXT. BELFRY/MEADOW. DAY

The landscape is radiant. MOON *emerges from his tent, looks up to belfry. Salutes* BIRKIN *cheerily.* BIRKIN *in long shot seen from* MOON's *point of view.*

INT. CHURCH. DAY

BIRKIN *on the scaffold. He is cleaning the last stages of the whole image of the falling man. We see him working on a detail, not clear what it is. He steps back and takes in the whole image. His face expresses controlled excitement. Cut to image. A crescent-shaped star on his brow, bright hair streaming like a torch (a second Simon Magus), plunging headlong down the wall. Two demons with delicately furred legs clutching him, one snapping his right wrist while his mate splits him with shears.*

BIRKIN: (*Mutters*) I wonder what you did then.
    (*The sound of footsteps below.* BIRKIN *is unaware.*)
MOSSOP: (*Out of shot*) Mr Birkin.
BIRKIN: (*Still engrossed*) Mmmmm?
MOSSOP: (*Out of shot*) Don't forget tha't standing umpire again this Sunday, Mr Birkin.
BIRKIN: What?
    (BIRKIN *turns and sees* MOSSOP.)
    Oh, no, I'm afraid I can't, Mossop, I've got an important engagement. (*Slightly maliciously*) You'll have to do it, I'm afraid.
MOSSOP: I can't neither, Mr Birkin. I'm busy too.
BIRKIN: Then it'll have to be the Colonel.
    (BIRKIN *turns back to the painting and we see again the falling man.*)

EXT. CROSSROADS. MORNING
Shot of crossroads, hot. Absolute stillness. BIRKIN *standing at it, his coat slung over his shoulder.* MOON *stands nearby. Their faces expectant, turning to look down one road, and then the next, and cut back to the crossroads. Then, almost inaudible at first, a clip-clop of horses' hoofs, growing louder and louder, cut back to their faces. Then, locating where sound is coming from, they look down the road, and there suddenly appear two flat-wheeled carts.* BIRKIN *and* MOON *are delighted. The horses glint with farthingales. The horses stop beside them. They climb into the first cart, which is less full.*

EDGAR: Mr Birkin, Mr Birkin!
>(BIRKIN *pauses, turns.*)
>You're with us.
>(KATHY *nods in agreement.* BIRKIN *moves to the second cart, sits between* KATHY *and* EDGAR, *across from the* ELLERBECKS *and others. In Moon's cart,* DOUTHWAITE, *his fingers in plaster, the blind man from the Post Office and several maimed men and* LUCY SYKES. MOON *sits next to* LUCY SYKES. *On the bench, the adults, the children sitting with their legs over the side of cart.* BIRKIN *squeezes in between the adults on the bench, then takes in* MOSSOP *sitting beside him, and evidently* MRS MOSSOP *beside* MOSSOP. MOSSOP *greets him with a nod.*)

BIRKIN: What are you doing with the chapel lot? You're church, aren't you?

MOSSOP: Nay. Ay've me fee at i'beath camps. The lot of 'em ha' git ti come at t'finish to let me put 'em ti bed.

EDGAR: (*Out of shot*) There she is, Mr Birkin.
>(*Cut to* EDGAR'*s face, serious, beside it* KATHY'*s grinning not entirely pleasantly.* EDGAR *pointing to the front cart, and as* BIRKIN *turns, sees at back of front cart,* LUCY SYKES *among the maimed men and next to* MOON, *who gestures triumphantly back at* BIRKIN. LUCY SYKES *from* BIRKIN'*s point of view, and then we see her cart, Birkin's cart, trundling through the countryside, idyllic.*)

EXT. FIELD BESIDE RIVER. DAY

Fire burning, kettle on it, and scattered around, the company, the
ELLERBECKS, *the* MOSSOPS, *and then* LUCY SYKES, *all from*
BIRKIN's *point of view as* DOUTHWAITE *by fire leads them in the*
doxology as: men without jackets larking around, younger men and
women in pairs talking, sidling off, EDGAR *off with other* BOYS
collecting sticks, the women sitting around talking, among them, to
one side LUCY SYKES *watching* MOON *as he demonstrates in mime*
how he intends with his rod to locate Piers's grave. The men begin to
leapfrog in background. BIRKIN *turns his head suddenly; we see*
beside him KATHY. KATHY *is looking towards* LUCY SYKES.

KATHY: What are you going to do now, Mr Birkin?
    (BIRKIN *sees* LUCY SYKES *glancing towards him. The men*
    playing leapfrog in the background begin to divert MOON's
    attention.)
BIRKIN: Why, talk to you of course, Miss Ellerbeck.
    (*Pause.*)
KATHY: What about?
BIRKIN: I don't know. But you usually have something to say
    about things.
KATHY: You'll be leaving soon, won't you?
BIRKIN: Well, as soon as I've finished.
KATHY: Why?
BIRKIN: Well, I'll have to go somewhere else where I can make
    a living.
    (BIRKIN *sees* MOON *say something to* LUCY SYKES *and with*
    a self-depreciating laugh run over to the leapfroggers and joins
    in. KATHY, *taking in that* LUCY SYKES *is now alone, more*
    urgently pursues her conversation with BIRKIN. LUCY *watches*
    MOON *leapfrogging, clearly aware of* BIRKIN.)
KATHY: My mam says she doesn't see how you *can* make a
    living at your job. She says there can't be all that many
    pictures hidden on walls.
BIRKIN: (*Grins.*) Well, it's true I don't make much of one.
KATHY: Well then, why don't you change your job and stay on
    at Oxgodby?
BIRKIN: Why?
KATHY: What?

BIRKIN: Why should I stay on in Oxgodby?

KATHY: My mam and dad have taken a liking to you, for one thing.

BIRKIN: What about you, do you think I should stay on?

KATHY: Lots of my friends would miss you. They like to think of you at your work. From the way I tell them about it. And I've told them about your roughing it up in the belfry, they like that too.

BIRKIN: But you still haven't answered for yourself. Why do *you* want me to stay?

KATHY: Anyway you're too late.

(BIRKIN *follows* KATHY's *gaze. Cut and see from his point of view and* KATHY's *a young man bending over* LUCY SYKES, *saying something.* LUCY SYKES *rises, goes off with the young man.* BIRKIN *turns to* KATHY, *who is grinning.* KATHY *runs off towards* EDGAR. *From* BIRKIN's *point of view we see* KATHY *running towards* EDGAR. *She turns, looks towards* LUCY SYKES *and the young man, who are walking off.* MOON, *in a state of great exhilaration, catches* BIRKIN's *eye and laughs wildly.* BIRKIN *smiles back. We take in* KATHY *and* EDGAR *watching, amazed.*)

EXT. COUNTRY ROADS. LATE AFTERNOON
Shot of the carriage returning in the dusk. LUCY SYKES *and the young man in first carriage. Also* MOON, *expression reflective, almost sad.* KATHY, EDGAR, MR *and* MRS ELLERBECK *in the second carriage with* BIRKIN *sitting opposite them.* ELLERBECK *asleep.* MRS ELLERBECK *with her arm around* EDGAR, *who is asleep.* KATHY, *her face set, seen from* BIRKIN's *point of view, clearly avoiding his gaze.* BIRKIN *continues to look at* KATHY, *who stares gravely back at him.* BIRKIN *smiles.* KATHY, *suddenly unable to help herself, grins, as the carriages come to a halt. Voices from the first carriage.* KATHY, *in an attempt to retrieve her dignity, looks away from* BIRKIN. *She looks serious as* MOSSOP *approaches the carriage.*

MOSSOP: It's Emily Clough. She died this afternoon.

(*Cut to* BIRKIN's *face, he looks towards* KATHY. *Cut to* KATHY's *face.* BIRKIN *looks towards* KATHY *as carriages start up. Cut to shot of carriages continuing down the road, around the bend, in the twilight. Fade on carriages disappearing.*)

INT. CHURCH. DAY
The COLONEL'*s face as he stands in nave looking at the mural.* BIRKIN *on the scaffold.* MOON *is with him. Both looking down. They both wait for the* COLONEL'*s response. He nods in approval and leaves.*

MOON: (*Turning to* BIRKIN) You're quite right. It's a masterpiece. I feel terribly smug, just the two of us knowing about it, before the *Times* art critic tips off the academic parasites. For the moment it's just ours – (MOON'*s face, cheerful.*)

BIRKIN: Look at this. (*Points to falling man.*) Have you ever seen a detail like it, in a medieval painting? It anticipates the Bruegels by a hundred years. And the face meant something to him. It's a portrait. It must be. And he was covered over years before the rest.

MOON: Yes, I see what you mean. The crescent scar. One could swear he was meant to be identifiable. But would he have dared, your painter? What was he like? You must know him pretty well by now.

BIRKIN: I can't even put a name to him, as he hasn't signed it. But then why would he? Our idea of personal f–f–fame meant nothing to him. (*Little pause*). But he was fair-haired. I know that from hairs that keep turning up where his beard prodded into the paint. He was right-handed, about your build – he had to use some sort of stool to get up to six feet. He probably lived in a monastery, because – well, look at the hands –
(*Cut to montage of hands.*)
– they talk to each other. Like monks' hands must have, during the long silences.
(*Montage of feet casually done.*)
The weird thing is he didn't finish the job himself. See this last bit –
(*Cut to corner of hell.*)
You can see it's a rough job. A fill-in. Probably done by his

apprentice. I can't imagine why – just when his nose was past the finishing post. And he knew that this was his great work. You can feel it, can't you?

(MOON *nods*.)

Whatever he'd been on before was only a run-up to this. He'd sweated here, tossed in his bed, g–g–groaned, howled over it –

(*Cut to Christ, his hands torn, fingers bent as if in agony*.) Those hands, those fingers.

(*Cut to* MOON.)

MOON: And he shal come with wondes rede, eh?

(MOON *turns away to leave. Cut to* BIRKIN'*s face as he turns back to the painting. Cut to the falling man. Sound over of* MOON'*s feet to which* BIRKIN *is oblivious. Sound of door squealing open.* BIRKIN *turns, suddenly realizing that* MOON *has gone. Then an expression of sudden realization as he looks down, and cut to the floor rising at him dizzyingly.* BIRKIN *looks towards the door,* MOON *just about to close it*.)

BIRKIN: (*Shouting*) Moon! Moon!

(MOON *turns*.)

He fell! (*Shouting*) That's why he didn't finish. It was his last job. He fell!

(MOON, *after a pause, grins*.)

MOON: OK. Mind your own step then.

(MOON *exits. Closes door*.)

EXT. TRAIN. DAY
Train racing across countryside.

INT. TRAIN COMPARTMENT. DAY
BIRKIN, ELLERBECK, KATHY, DOUTHWAITE, *all at their most respectably dressed,* KATHY *with a package on her lap*.

ELLERBECK: Ah, but, Mr Birkin. You've a real eye for quality. That anybody can tell. And we want the best. Well, put it this way (*nods*) we want the best we can afford.

EXT. TRAIN. DAY
Train hurtling along.

EXT. STREET. DAY
Market stalls up and down the street. BIRKIN, ELLERBECK,
DOUTHWAITE *and* KATHY *crossing through stalls towards a shop,
in long shot, entering.*

INT. SHOP: BACKROOM. DAY
Directly in on a YOUNG MAN.

YOUNG MAN: You'd better have a look behind that lot over
    there. (*Gestures.*) We took them in part exchange.
DOUTHWAITE: I suppose it's in order to try one or two out?
    (*The sound of the door opening; the bell rings. The* YOUNG
    MAN *turns towards it, as we hear the sound of people entering.*)

INT. SHOP. LATER. DAY

ELLERBECK: That's settled then. One of these three. Kathy
    lass, try them out.
    (KATHY, *sitting at an organ, playing 'All People that on Earth
    do Dwell' and cut to her at another organ playing 'All People
    that on Earth do Dwell' and to the third organ playing 'All
    People that on Earth do Dwell'; on each occasion*
    DOUTHWAITE *listening with his head to the organ's back.*)
DOUTHWAITE: (*As the third organ comes to silence*) I'm no
    musician, Mr Birkin. That I freely admit to. But wind, that
    I do understand.
ELLERBECK: What do you think, Mr Birkin?
BIRKIN: Well, um – that one vibrates. And that one smells odd.
ELLERBECK: (*Indicating the third organ*) Then this is the one we
    test. To the limit. Kathy, lass.
    (KATHY *arranges herself at the organ, raises her hands to start.
    Sudden peals of thunder, fanfares from the front of shop.*)
KATHY: Go inquire how long he's going to make that din for,
    Mr Birkin.
    (BIRKIN *hesitates, turns, and as the music from front
    continues, goes through the aisle of organs to the front of shop.*)

INT. SHOP FRONT. DAY

As BIRKIN *reaches the front, the shop door opens and* YOUNG
WOMAN *holds it open for young man who enters on crutches –*
MILBURN. *He has only one leg. The organ music stops. Cut to*
YOUNG MAN, MR *and* MRS KEACH *around the organ, and then
focus on* MRS KEACH *listening to the* YOUNG MAN, *his voice
murmuring politely, over, seen from* BIRKIN'S *point of view. In
periphery* MILBURN *and* YOUNG WOMAN *have gone over to
inspect some flutes.* BIRKIN, *transfixed, and then to* MRS KEACH,
stay on her face, bending to listen, as, abruptly over, the voices of
KATHY, ELLERBECK, DOUTHWAITE *raised in hymn, organ
playing: 'Worthy is the Lamb / Worthy is the Lamb / Worthy is the
Lamb for sinners slain'.* MRS KEACH, *smiling looks towards the
sound, sees* BIRKIN. KEACH *looks up bewildered. The* YOUNG
MAN *looks up in irritation.* MILBURN *and* YOUNG WOMAN *look
first bewildered, then laugh.*

VOICES: (*Out of shot*) For Sinners slai–i–i–in / Worthy is the
Lamb for sinners slai–i–i–in.
(BIRKIN *stands in the room as the hymn continues, then
suddenly stops. There is a pause.*)

MILBURN: (*To the* YOUNG WOMAN) I must say I much prefer
the jolly hymns.
(ELLERBECK *and* DOUTHWAITE *enter the front,* KATHY
following.)

ELLERBECK: (*As he enters, to the* YOUNG MAN) That's it then,
we'll have the Auberdech.

DOUTHWAITE: Any discount for cash? (*Taking out a heap of
cash*) Let's say a couple of pounds off, cash down, shall we?
(MILBURN *and the* YOUNG WOMAN *obviously enjoying this.*
MILBURN *suddenly becoming slightly aware of* BIRKIN.)

ELLERBECK: And to include delivery, of course.

YOUNG MAN: Where to?

DOUTHWAITE: Oxgodby.
(*Throughout this* BIRKIN *is conscious of* MRS KEACH.)

EXT. MARKET. DAY
KATHY, ELLERBECK, DOUTHWAITE, BIRKIN, *emerging from the shop.* BIRKIN *glancing into the shop at* MRS KEACH, *her face half turned towards him, but noticing that* MILBURN *is watching him.*

DOUTHWAITE: Well, that's a neat little bit of business neatly done. Four pounds off plus delivery.
ELLERBECK: We'll have to move a bit if we're going to catch the four seven.
KATHY: That's Mrs Keach, you know, with the vicar. (*To* BIRKIN) Have you met her yet?
DOUTHWAITE: Come on then. Let's get going.
BIRKIN: Actually I'd quite like to have a look at the church as I'm here.
(*Cut to* KATHY's *face looking at him suspiciously as* BIRKIN *glances back into the window and we see from his point of view* MRS KEACH. *He is still not really aware of* MILBURN *who is watching him.*)

INT./EXT. TEASHOP/ORGAN SHOP/MARKET. DAY
BIRKIN *has a cup of tea before him, but is staring through the teashop window into the organ-shop window, through which he can make out the shapes of* KEACH *and* MRS KEACH, *and the* YOUNG MAN *in conference. We see him first, then them from his point of view.* MR *and* MRS KEACH *come through shop door, on to the pavement, confer briefly. They separate,* MRS KEACH *going to a stall to the left of* BIRKIN's *vision, but staying in vision.* KEACH *going to stalls on right of* BIRKIN's *vision. Cut to shot of* MRS KEACH *selecting apples. Cut to shot of* KEACH *bent over, studying the fish. See his face in relation to the fish, fastidiously selecting some plaice. During this* MILBURN *comes out on the pavement with the* YOUNG WOMAN. *Spots* BIRKIN *in the teashop. Stands on the pavement, explaining something to the* YOUNG WOMAN. *Cut back to* MRS KEACH, *a bag of apples in her hand.* MRS KEACH *takes an apple out, bites it. As she does so, she sees* BIRKIN. *She smiles. Cut to* BIRKIN's *face, smiling back at her. Cut back to* MRS KEACH. *She makes as if to move towards him.* KEACH *appears beside her, carrying fish wrapped.* MILBURN *says something to the* YOUNG WOMAN, *touches her on the arm, heads towards the shop, unnoticed*

by BIRKIN. KEACH *says something to* MRS KEACH, *looks down at
the fish.* MRS KEACH *looks over towards* BIRKIN *as sound of the
teashop door opening, over.*

MILBURN: Excuse me.
   (BIRKIN *looks up.*)
   You're from Oxgodby.
BIRKIN: Yes, well, just visiting.
MILBURN: Have you bumped into a chap called Moon over
   there. Charles Moon. Digging up some field or something.
BIRKIN: Yes. I have.
MILBURN: And is he a short, round-faced, curly-haired pink
   sort of chap? Smiles a lot?
BIRKIN: (*Smiling*) That's pretty well him, yes.
MILBURN: A Captain in the Eighteenth Norfolk Artillery?
BIRKIN: Yes.
MILBURN: Well, that clinches it, doesn't it? Must be the same
   chap. Would you give him a salute from me?
BIRKIN: Of course.
MILBURN: And from all the other officers of the Eighteenth
   Norfolk. The ones who didn't sit out the last six months in
   the glasshouse. For buggering their batman.
   (MILBURN, *nods, turns, limps out.*)

INT./EXT. TENT. DAY
MOON *and* BIRKIN *sitting outside the tent drinking tea. Cut to*
MOON *glancing at* BIRKIN. BIRKIN *abstracted.* MOON *smiles
affectionately.*

MOON: It agrees with you, doesn't it?
BIRKIN: What does?
MOON: Oxgodby. Since you've been here they've almost gone,
   your ticks and twitch and stammer.
BIRKIN: Yes, I suppose they have. I hadn't noticed.
MOON: And what about the vicar's lovely lady? Have you seen
   anything of her?
BIRKIN: No, not really.
MOON: A pity.
BIRKIN: Is it?

MOON: (*Laughs.*) No, probably not. Much better off without it, aren't we? If we want an easy life.
(BIRKIN *lifts his mug, smiles at* MOON.)
BIRKIN: Well, here's to an easy life.

EXT./INT. LANDSCAPES/PAINTING. MONTAGE
Sweeping shots of village, meadow, graveyard, etc. Mingling shots of above with shots of paradise from the painting, to make up an actual and an ideal landscape into one, but ending on paradise section in picture.

> *Wide shot of landscape near church, in sun/rain/dawn/dusk*
> *Fields in heat haze*
> *Tent in the meadow in heat haze*
> *Dew on the meadow*
> *Rain on the leaves*
> *Birds/bees/butterflies*
> *Sheep*
> *Horses*
> *Trees*
> *Threshing machine/work*
> *Headstones in the moonlight*
> *Sound: moorland before sunset; dawn chorus*

INT. CHURCH. DAY
The face of MR KEACH, *on the scaffold, observing the finished picture and faces of the saved. The sound of the door squealing open, footsteps. Cut to* BIRKIN *below, seen from* KEACH'S *point of view on the scaffold. Cut to* KEACH *climbing down the ladder.*

KEACH: Mossop told me you'd finished. And I can see you have. Very good. In accordance with the executors' wishes, here is the final payment from Miss Hebron's estate.
(*At the bottom,* KEACH *hands* BIRKIN *an envelope.*)
Thirteen pounds fifteen shillings, as was agreed.
BIRKIN: What do you think of it?
KEACH: (*Vaguely*) Mmmm?
BIRKIN: The painting. What do you think of it?
(KEACH *looks vaguely towards it.*)

KEACH: Well, it's there. So you've done the job you were contracted for. And now you've been paid.

BIRKIN: (*After a slight pause*) Thank you. Of course I'll need the scaffolding for several more days.

KEACH: Why?

BIRKIN: Because I haven't finished.

KEACH: What remains to be done?

BIRKIN: That's for me to decide.

KEACH: I shall have the scaffolding removed.

BIRKIN: Oh, will you? Then I shall inform the executors that you've prevented me from completing my work, which will relieve them of the obligation to contribute the thousand pounds to your fabric fund, won't it?

KEACH: (*After a slight pause*) I should not wish to quarrel with you, Mr Birkin.

(BIRKIN *nods.* KEACH *turns to go, then turns back, looks at* BIRKIN. BIRKIN *waits.*)

Oh, I know how you see me, Mr Birkin. The way you want to. You and Mr Moon. And all the people in this parish. My parish. You've never thought what it's like for a man like me, have you? The English are not a deeply religious people. Most of those who attend divine service do so only from habit. Their acceptance of the sacrament is perfunctory. I have yet to meet the man whose hair rose at the nape of his neck because he was about to taste the blood of his dying Lord. Would I find such a man in Oxgodby? When they come to my church in large numbers, at Harvest Thanksgiving or the Christmas Midnight Mass, it's no more than a pagan salute to the passing of the seasons. They do not need me, they merely find me useful at baptisms, weddings, funerals. Chiefly funerals. Because I help see to the orderly disposal of their dead. (*Laughs bitterly.*) But I'm embarrassing you, Mr Birkin. And embarrassing people is a real sin, isn't it? For one thing it makes them see us slightly differently. (*Makes to say something else, checks himself.*) If you could let me know when I may have the scaffolding dismantled.

(*Cut to* BIRKIN's *face, as, over, the sound of* KEACH's *footsteps, the door squealing.*)

EXT. GRAVEYARD WALL. MORNING
*At the subsidence by the graveyard wall, by them a bag, a shovel,
an old wooden box, a camera,* MOON *holding a long steel shaft.*

MOON: Oh, come off it, Birkin, of course Keach is right. You
　　　have finished. If one couldn't tell by looking at the wall,
　　　one can tell by looking at your face. You can't keep
　　　munching at this piece of cake for ever. Here. (*Hands
　　　diviner to* BIRKIN.) Excommunicate or not my Piers was
　　　important enough to rate a stone box. Push it into the
　　　earth. There. Do you feel it?
BIRKIN: (*Pushing it in*) No.
MOON: Well, then – do it again a few inches further on. And so
　　　forth. Until you hit it. (*Little pause, grins.*) Off you go. I'll
　　　take over when we'll need a professional touch.
　　　(*Cut to* MOON *some time later, further on, probing delicately.
　　　Cut to* BIRKIN *watching him. Cut back to* MOON, *stopping
　　　suddenly.*)
BIRKIN: What is it?
MOON: Either a boulder deeper than it ought to be, or the lid of
　　　a stone coffin perhaps.
　　　(MOON *puts down diviner, picks up shovel, slight pause, hands
　　　it to* BIRKIN.)
　　　Do you know what this is for?

EXT. HEBRON'S GRAVE. DAY
Montage. Cut to BIRKIN *digging in the heat. Twelve inches down
and sweating.* MOON *sitting on the box watching.* BIRKIN, *shirt
off, two feet down. Low up to wall.* MOSSOP *and scythe leaning
against it. School bell ringing.* MOSSOP *eating his lunch off the
wall. Low up to* MOON *sitting smoking his pipe. A crescent of school
children, including* KATHY, *around them. They gradually disperse.*

MOON: A true-blue British workman, eh? Mr Mossop?
　　　(MOSSOP, *lunch finished, sitting on the wall. He looks dour
　　　and sceptical as he moves away, muttering.* BIRKIN *digging in
　　　the heat as the hole gets deeper.*)
　　　(*Out of shot*) Doesn't it excite you? Digging where someone
　　　dug five, six hundred years ago?

(BIRKIN, *sweating profusely, glances towards him.*)
Oh, well, you're spoiled. You clean a wall and find a
masterpiece. You turn over the earth and expect to find a
pot of gold. But we diggers keep our palates fresh. A mild
deviation of tinge is all we need – (*moving towards* BIRKIN)
– to stir the adrenalin. (*Holds out his hand for the spade.*)
Haven't you noticed that you're throwing up soil that
should have been three spits deeper?
(MOON *is troweling earth into the bag almost full. Signals.*
BIRKIN *draws it up, dumps it. Cut to* MOON *holding up an
object.*)
Horn button. Fifteenth century.
(MOON *tosses it up.* BIRKIN *catches it.*)
(*Out of shot*) Right on target.
(*Cut to* MOON. *He is brushing away with his hands with rapid
strokes, barefooted. Cut back to* BIRKIN *watching him,
crouching. Moon's socks and shoes beside him, and then back to*
MOON, *close in on his hands brushing the earth, then back to*
BIRKIN *his face expressing excitement, and then back to*
MOON's *hands, uncovering the stone so that it swims into sight.
A carved shaft branching gracefully into whorls of stone raised
upon a convex lid. At its head a hand holding a sacramental
cup. Wafer poised at its rim.* MOON *stops brushing when it's
completely revealed, peers. Cut to* BIRKIN.)
BIRKIN: Well? Come on. Is it Piers or isn't it?
(*Cut to* MOON *peering down.*)
MOON: Just 'Miserisimus'. I of all men the most wretched.
They really had it in for the poor devil. (*Looking up, his
face dirty.*) Didn't they? I wonder why. Ah well, I suppose
we'll never know.
(*Cut to* MOON *taking photographs from different angles,
succession of shots.*)
For publication. Against the day when I need a university
job. (*Putting down camera*) They don't want to know if
you've been anywhere, seen or done anything, just what
you've published. (*Turns. Grinning*) Shall we have a peep
inside?
(*Cut to* MOON, BIRKIN *in the pit.* BIRKIN *pushing,* MOON
pulling at lid, then cut to shot of the coffin, seen from above as

*lid swivels slowly off. Revealed, a skeleton, full length. Stay
on it.)*
(Out of shot) Look – see it. Third rib down.
*(Close in on something metal swinging glintingly behind the rib
cage. Cut to golden crescent, on a chain, in* MOON's *hand. Cut
to* MOON's *face, looking down, then to* BIRKIN's *looking
down, then back to crescent.)*
Miserisimus.

INT. CHURCH. DAY
BIRKIN *and* MOON *on scaffold. Cut to face of falling man on wall,
crescent of forehead evident.*

MOON: He was a converted Muslim. Caught on some Christian
Crusade, I suppose, and converted to save his skin.
Imagine the ructions in Oxgodby when he turned up again
and was still worshipping to the East.
*(Little pause as we take in the two demons clutching him, one
snapping his right wrist, one splitting him with shears, his face
in torment.)*
Both our mysteries solved.
BIRKIN: Well, it was the same mystery, wasn't it?

INT. BELFRY. AFTERNOON
MRS KEACH *appears at the trapdoor. In her hat a rose, a Sarah van
Fleet. We see her from* BIRKIN's *point of view then cut to him
looking at her. He is sitting, smoking on the bed.*

MRS KEACH: I hear you've finished.
BIRKIN: Yes.
MRS KEACH: I've brought you a bag of apples. To say goodbye
with.
(She holds out bag. BIRKIN *takes it.)*
BIRKIN: Thank you.
MRS KEACH: They're Ribston Pippins. They do well up here.
Exactly the right soil and climate. Lots of other varieties
don't take, though.
BIRKIN: You're an expert in apples, then, are you?
MRS KEACH: I am. My father taught me. Before he bit into one

he'd sniff it, roll it around his cupped palms, then smell his hands. Then he'd tap and finger it like a blind man. Sometimes he made me close my eyes and when I'd had a bite he'd ask me to say which apple. So this is where you've been living all this time.

(MRS KEACH *looking around, observed by* BIRKIN, *as she takes in lamp, kitbag, camp bed. She picks up Scott-Bradshaw's* A History of Church Architecture, *glances at cover, makes to open it, doesn't. A pause between them.* MRS KEACH *still holding the book. She crosses to window, looks out.* BIRKIN *watches her.*)

(*Looking out of the window*) And there's Mr Moon.

BIRKIN: (*Watching her*) Yes.

(*As if coming to a decision,* BIRKIN *walks over to the window beside her. They are pressing against each other, side against side.* MOON, *seen from their point of view sitting outside his tent, scribbling and drawing.* BIRKIN *turns towards* MRS KEACH. *She turns towards* BIRKIN. *They straighten. They stand staring at each other.*)

He's dug up the bones he was commissioned to dig up. And turned up an Anglo-Saxon basilica in the process. The basilica is what he really came for. He knew it was here.

MRS KEACH: Oh. Bones and a basilica.

BIRKIN: Yes.

MRS KEACH: (*Nods.*) So you've both found what you came to find?

(*Cut from her face to his. He makes to say something, doesn't. There is a pause.*)

I'm glad.

(*Little pause. She turns to go. Cut to* MRS KEACH's *face. Hat. Sarah van Fleet rose. Cut from rose to* MRS KEACH *walking across the steps. Begins to go down. Stops. Smiles.*)

Your book.

BIRKIN: Oh.

(*He goes over, takes it from her.*)

INT. BELFRY STEPS. DAY

MRS KEACH *descending the steps.*

INT. BELFRY. DAY
BIRKIN *standing, holding book. Sound of footsteps below, the door squealing open, squealing shut.*

INT. BELFRY/NAVE. EVENING
BIRKIN *sitting with his back against the wall. The book beside him, open. See rose. Twilight through the window. Below, distantly and over, the sound of the door squealing open. Footsteps.* BIRKIN *rises, goes to steps, looks down. From his point of view the nave empty. Sound of footsteps approaching beneath.* KATHY *appears. Turns her face up towards him.*

KATHY: (*Calling upwards*) Mr Birkin – Mr Birkin –
   (*Stay on* KATHY *as she looks around, from* BIRKIN'S *point of view then she turns, walks away. Sound of footsteps, door opening with a squeal, closing.*)

INT. BELFRY. EVENING
Later. BIRKIN *gets up, leaves belfry.*

EXT. VICARAGE. NIGHT
BIRKIN *approaches, looks at the lit windows, hears the violin, turns and goes.*

INT. CHURCH. MORNING
BIRKIN *finishes packing his tools with great energy.* MOON *arrives at the door, dressed for departure.*

MOON: (*Cheerfully*) A letter. The postman asked me to drop it 'up'.
BIRKIN: Thank you. (*Looks at it.*) From Vinny. My wife. Probably wanting us to start over again. She usually does.
MOON: And will you?
BIRKIN: (*Wryly*) I usually do.
   (BIRKIN *looks at* MOON.)
   And where are you off to?
   (*He grins.*)
MOON: Basra – Baghdad. There's a big dig going on there. I'd like to get in on it.

BIRKIN: Right.

MOON: What about you?

BIRKIN: Don't know. Wait for another church, I suppose.

MOON: You'll never get another one like this.

BIRKIN: I know. (*Little pause.*) It's been a summer, hasn't it?
  (MOON *nods. There is a pause.*)

MOON: So.
  (MOON *looks vaguely around, then back towards* BIRKIN. *Cut
  to* BIRKIN's *face. Cut back to* MOON. *Slight pause.*)
  Well.
  (*He holds out his hand.* BIRKIN *takes it. They shake hands.
  Cut to* MOON, *from* BIRKIN's *point of view at the belfry
  window, walking jauntily across and out of frame, carrying
  bags, etc.* BIRKIN *turns away, takes coat off hook.*)

INT. CHURCH NAVE. MORNING

BIRKIN *stopping at the catafalque. Laetitia, and the lettering:
'Conjugam Optimam Amantissima et Delectissima – ' Cut to*
BIRKIN's *face, smiling slightly. He places* MRS KEACH's *rug on the
tomb.* BIRKIN, *take him in full shot. He is turning away from the
catafalque and is as when he arrived, carrying his kit, etc., but with
his coat over his arm. He turns, looks towards the wall-painting.
The scaffolding is still up,* BIRKIN's *view of the painting obscured.
He hesitates, as if about to go towards it. Turns, walks down the
nave towards door, his footsteps clapping. Opens door. It squeals.*

EXT. MEADOW/GRAVEYARD. DAY

BIRKIN *walking across the meadow. He reaches into one of his
bags, takes out an apple, bites on it. Eats.* MOON, *his tent, all sign
of his occupancy gone. The day is almost sunless, windy. Horse and
cart labouring across a corner of the meadow. Stay on* BIRKIN
*walking away, eating an apple as suddenly the sound of a hymn 'As
Pants the Heart' thinly but distinctly.* BIRKIN *stops, turns, the
apple halfway to his mouth, looking towards church.*

EXT./INT. CHURCH. DAY

The church from BIRKIN's *point of view, cars parked, modern. An*
OLD MAN, *carrying a book, walking with a stick, approaches
church door. The hymn continues. The* OLD MAN *watches the*

sparse, singing congregation. He is standing at the back. In his hand, an old book, possibly the Scott-Bradshaw A History of Church Architecture, *but the title is not distinct. The* OLD MAN *lifts his eyes from the congregation to the wall-painting, which slowly fills the screen as the hymn is replaced by magnificent music.* BIRKIN *crossing field, eating apple, and back again to wall-painting, back to* BIRKIN, *as music continues and finally fading from* BIRKIN *to the wall-painting.*